DIRTY STOP OUTS GUIDE TO 1980s Chesterfield AQUARIUS Edition

By Neil Anderson

Aquarius favourite Bob Monkhouse (third from left) with John Williamson (left), Tufty Gordon (second from right) and George Nafu (right)

Starring:

Brampton Mile   Connection Records   Painted Wagon   Adam & Eve
Fascination   Hudsons   Moulin Rouge   Three Horse Shoes

and many more!

Derbyshire Times

All rights reserved. No part of this book may be reproduced in any form or by any electronic or mechanical means, including information storage or retrieval systems, without permission in writing from the publisher, except by a reviewer who may quote brief passages.
Every effort has been made to trace the copyright holders of photographers in this book but one or two were unreachable. We would be grateful if the photographers concerned would contact us.

Neil Anderson asserts the moral right
to be identified as the author of this work.
A catalogue record for this book is available from the British Library.

Published by ACM Retro

Please note that a large part of this book was originally published in 2013 as the Dirty Stop Out's Guide to 1980s Chesterfield.

Other titles in this series:

Dirty Stop Out's Guide to 1970s Manchester.

Dirty Stop Out's Guide to 1970s Liverpool.

Dirty Stop Out's Guide to 1970s Coventry.

Dirty Stop Out's Guide to 1970s Barnsley.

Dirty Stop Out's Guide to 1950s Sheffield.

Dirty Stop Out's Guide to 1960s Sheffield.

Dirty Stop Out's Guide to 1970s Sheffield.

Dirty Stop Out's Guide to 1980s Sheffield.

Dirty Stop Out's Guide to 1980s Sheffield – King Mojo Edition

Dirty Stop Out's Guide to 1990s Sheffield.

Dirty Stop Out's Guide to 1970s Chesterfield.

Dirty Stop Out's Guide to 1970s Sheffield – Club Fiesta Edition.

Dirty Stop Out's Guide to 1980s Chesterfield.

Dirty Stop Out's Guide to 1980s Coventry.

Dirty Stop Out's Guide to 1980s Sheffield – The Limit Edition

Dirty Stop Out's Guide to 1980s Chesterfield Quizbook.

Dirty Stop Out's Guide to 1990s Chesterfield

We're on the look out for writers to cover other UK towns and cities and we're always on the look out for great retro photos!
Please email us at info@dirtystopouts.com if you fancy getting involved.

www.dirtystopouts.com

DiRTY STOP OUTS GUIDE to 1980s Chesterfield
AQUARIUS Edition

By Neil Anderson

Starring:

Brampton Mile   **Connection Records**   **Painted Wagon**   **Adam & Eve**
Fascination   **Hudsons**   **Moulin Rouge**   **Three Horse Shoes**

and many more!

Derbyshire Times

NORMAN COLLIER
Agent: DOROTHY SOLOMON ASSOCIATED ARTISTES LTD
PICCADILLY HOUSE, 33 LOWER REGENT STREET
LONDON SW1Y 4NE
Telephone 01 734 9768

Jimmy Ruffin
New single "Thank You Girl" 2058 901
New album "Jimmy Ruffin" 2383 240

polydor
MARKETED BY POLYDOR LIMITED

Some of the many stars that performed at the Aquarius

Dirty Stop Outs Guide to **1980s** Chesterfield **AQUARIUS** Edition

★〰️ CONTENTS

★ **Introduction - Dawn of a Sheffield Road after dark legend**

Chapter 1
★ The Aquarius - "It was a special, special place"

Chapter 2
★ Thompson Twins to the rescue

Chapter 3
★ 'Video nasties' from Chesterfield Co-op

Chapter 4
★ Mullets and more for the masses

Chapter 5
★ Live Aid comes to town

Chapter 6
★ Alternative comedy and a home for Henry Normal

Chapter 7
★ The Brampton Mile - a true rite of passage

Chapter 8
★ From the Spasms to the Septic Psychos - town's own music heroes

Chapter 9
★ Home entertainment was the stuff of nightmares for the hapless house party host

Chapter 10
★ A night at the 'Acca'

Dirty Stop Outs Guide to **1980s** Chesterfield **AQUARIUS** Edition

An 1980s beauty contest at the Aquarius

Dirty Stop Outs Guide to **1980s** Chesterfield **AQUARIUS** Edition

Dirty Stop Outs Guide to **1980s** Chesterfield **AQUARIUS** Edition

The Anchor pool team toast their trophy cabinet

Chesterfield vinyl institution Connection Records

DAWN OF AN AFTER DARK LEGEND

Iconic faces of the Aquarius

Nightlife is a notoriously fickle business. But one Chesterfield operation outlasted scores of its peers and provided memories that will be cherished by tens of thousands of its former regulars for years to come.

Sheffield Road's Aquarius opened on the back of the rise of the glitzy cabaret movement which swept the country in the late 1960s.

The demand for stylish, sophisticated venues was massive.

The Fiesta opened in Sheffield in the summer of 1970 – hot on the heels of the Cavendish which opened a couple of years earlier. The Fiesta set the gold standard for much of the country – it was the biggest nightclub in the whole of Europe when it was unveiled.

At the same time the Working Men's Club scene was exploding with massive investment as they unveiled shiny new concert rooms and more. They became the training ground for many of the acts that went on to achieve their dream and perform on the more glitzy and prestigious cabaret circuit – the Aquarius eventually becoming a key destination.

The early seventies was an affluent period for Chesterfield and the UK generally. Punters wanted a better quality night out.

Dirty Stop Outs Guide to **1980s** Chesterfield   **AQUARIUS** Edition

A night in the cabaret room

AQUARIUS NIGHT CLUB
SHEFFIELD ROAD, CHESTERFIELD TEL: 70188/9
V.A.T. Reg. No. 295 3646 22

A 3808 TABLE No. 9

No. of Persons ....

STARTERS
Prawn Cocktail ....
Fruit or Tomato Juice ....
Minestrone ....
Grapefruit Cocktail ....
Smoked Salmon ....
Pate Maison ....

MAIN COURSE   *Paid*
Fillet Steak ....
Sirloin Steak ....

HOUSE SPECIALITY
Chicken ....
Gammon Steak ....
Scampi ....
Turkey ....

SWEETS
Gateaux ....
Apple Pie ....
Ice Cream ....
Cheese ....
Coffee ....

A   3808   £

Enjoying a night out

Aquarius revellers

The Aquarius was perfectly poised to deliver it as it was unveiled in 1972.

It was a virtual overnight success as acts queued up to perform. Nightlife seemed to revolve around the place for much of the era.

Wedding receptions, hen parties, stag nights, birthday parties, office nights out – there was little that wasn't accommodated by the Aquarius.

> **Sue Ellis:**
> "I seemed to be at the Acca every single weekend for much of the 1980s. It was the place to go. I met my husband to be there – and we still kept going even after we got married as all our friends were there!"

By the end of the 1970s the world had changed. Cabaret was starting to fall out of favour, punk was snarling its way into the charts and 'Saturday Night Fever' was dragging the UK population onto the dancefloor without the need for a headline act on the stage.

The business model that had supported venues like Batley Variety Club and the Fiesta was now dead in the water.

Sheffield's Fiesta shut for the last time in 1980.

The Aquarius was a different animal. It reinvented itself and thrived for the majority of the 1980s – led by its disco.

It continued to be a massive pull for the whole region as coaches continued to make the weekly pilgrimage to the nightspot. The next generation of nightowls quickly adopted it.

Cowboys and country at the Aquarius

The Aquarius meant many things for many people. In August 1980 Neil Atkin headlined it – he remembers it as one of the highpoints of his life. It was another first for his family.

He said: "My dad was David H. Lee, a country music singer who had a minor hit in America in 1971. In a previous incarnation he had been `Dave Darby – the Singing Cowboy' and in 1958 became the first Chesterfield-born man to appear on national television when he won a TV talent show called `Bid For Fame' hosted by MacDonald Hobley on ITV.

In 1979 & 1980 he had a 12 show series on Border TV and was voted Top Male Solo Artiste in the Country Music Awards.

At the time I was his manager, and had changed my name from Neil Atkin to Neil Lee. I fronted a country music trio known as Reb Lee Colt & The Outlaws.

At the time I lived just 300 metres from the Aquarius, and went to see the manager, John Williamson to see if we could audition for a spot at the club.

He only dealt with agencies so I asked about the possibility of hiring the club on a Monday, (when normally it would be closed) with the idea of putting on one of our `Country Music Spectaculars' – and we agreed a deal. I had to organise and comperé the show and do a couple of spots with `the Outlaws'. I contacted the leading Country Music mag, `Country Music Round-up' and arranged with the Editor to have the Country Music Annual Awards Night at the Aquarius on August 11th 1980 and the joint editors and owners, Ma & Pa Kettle agreed to present the awards.

By the time I kicked off the show there was an audience of around 900. Everything went like clockwork; best male solo – David H Lee; best trio – Misty Mountain; best country band – Hombre; best country music DJ – Paul `Grizzly' Wasley; best newcomer – Reb Lee Colt & the Outlaws (performing their new single, `Whiskey Sundown' – and the Derbyshire Quick Draw Competition was won by `Doc Twigg (who by the time he collected his award on stage around midnight, was so pissed he fell off and demolished two tables of drinks!)

"It was a magical experience and I think I was the first local man to top the bill at the club – even before Bernie Clifton!"

> **By the time I kicked off the show there was an audience of around 900. Everything went like clockwork**

Marti Caine – a popular face at the Aquarius

Below: David H. Lee (second from right) with his son Neil Atkin (left) and Ma & Pa Kettle – joint editors of Country Music Round-up

THE AQUARIUS -
"IT WAS A SPECIAL, SPECIAL PLACE."

Chesterfield really had seen nothing like the venue when it opened its doors for the first time. Anticipation had been building for months as the building took shape and people queued up for the possibility of landing a a job at the prestigious new club.

The venue was the brainchild of Mr J. D. Williamson senior. His son, Mr John Williamson, became involved from an early age and became the face of the venue in later years.

Mr Williamson senior had forged a strong relationship with Mansfield Brewery, and it was that partnership that helped create the venue that was to become the Aquarius.

Punchbowl Entertainments was the name of the business. It was actually rooted in Skegness where Mr Williamson senior operated various ventures on the East Coast – he even became Lord Mayor of the town.

> Nobody was in the thick of the action more than Aquarius compère and all round showman, Chesterfield's own Bernie Clifton

He also had a major love of Spain – which was the inspiration for much of the design of the inside and outside of the Aquarius.

Nobody was in the thick of the action more than Aquarius compère and all round showman, Chesterfield's own Bernie Clifton, in its early days.

His career was on vertical trajectory and much of it was played out on home turf.

Bernie Clifton remembers: "In 1973 I was already doing quite well on the cabaret circuit and I used to compère at Batley Variety Club and I used to sing a lot. But then something happened to my voice and I

New compere for Aquarius

Starting on Sunday "Aquarius" will have a new resident compere, Bernie Clifton, as reported last week.

After several years, Bernie has now established himself as one of the leading comedy entertainers on the Northern Clubland Circuit.

His recent t.v. appearances included a spot on the B.B.C. Television show, "The Good Old Days," and as a result of his success on the show, he took part in the stage version at the Winter Gardens, Blackpool, last summer.

Bernie is no stranger to compering, having just completed a season at the world famous Batley Variety Club with such names as Shirley Bassey, Jack Jones and Freddie Starr.

Enjoying a night out

turned into a monotone. It was something to do with the nodules on my vocal chords and I had to stop work. It happened at a time that Eddie Buchanan, who had been compere at the Fiesta, had just left. It was like fate as I just fell into the job and I lived 100 yards away from the stage door. I used to leave my house, walk through the neighbour's garden and I was in the Aquarius carpark. I had to rest my voice for three months and I worked at the Aquarius through the summer of 1973. But as a result of that, John Williamson the Aquarius owner, offered me the job of booking the acts. I used to work above the Blue Bell pub which used to be the base for Punchbowl Entertainments. I was in the office

Margaret Fox: "Marti Cane propping the bar up, love her, scampi or chicken in a basket while watching a show, had some fabulous stars on stage even the late but great Bob Monkhouse, The Krankies and the hypnotist! Too many to mention then off for a dance later. Happy days."

"I remember booking Cannon and Ball, it was £300. They turned up for the band call on the Sunday afternoon and were horrified to find they were topping the bill.

all day on the phone to the London agents. I'd then go home, have my tea and it would be down to the Aquarius. I did that for about nine months.

"I remember booking Cannon and Ball, it was £300. They turned up for the band call on the Sunday afternoon and were horrified to find they were topping the bill. They were quaking in their boots and they said they'd never topped a bill before. They said 'we're a support act'. We took a chance because we knew how popular they were. They ended up topping the bill and went down a storm.

"It was a special, special place.

"I always remember Bernard Manning coming. It was a Rotary Club function which would quite often happen on a Monday or a Tuesday. They'd booked it months in advance without knowing the

AQUARIUS Night Club
A Complete Night Out

HOT AND COLD BUFFET LUNCHES Monday - Friday
2 Resident Groups SPANISH LOUNGE ZODIAC DISCO

THIS WEEK

LITTLE and LARGE
Martyn Wilson
Duo Saffron

W/C April 4 — PAUL DANIELS
Monday, April 5 Chesterfield Mayor's Appeal, In aid of Mentally Handicapped Children Fashion Show

W/C April 11 — MARTI CAINE
Monday, April 12 Boxing Tournament, Meal & Cabaret
W/C April 18 — BLACK ABBOTS
Easter Sunday Easter Bonnet Parade Cash Prizes (Open Easter Monday)

W/C April 25 — SACHA DISTEL
(Open Monday)
W/C MAY 2 — DUGGIE BROWN
May 4 and 5 only — THE DRIFTERS

★ Sheffield Road, CHESTERFIELD. Tel: 70188/9 ★

Dirty Stop Outs Guide to **1980s** Chesterfield   **AQUARIUS** Edition

CABARET WINE & DINE — AQUARIUS Night Club — SPANISH LOUNGE ZODIAC DISCO

THIS WEEK
Rockin' Berries
LES DENNIS
FOCUS HARMONY
Full supporting show
NEXT WEEK
IVY BENSON
SHOWBAND
10th and 11th December
Zodiac Room closed till 12 p.m.

CHRISTMAS CRACKER SHOW
Matinees 2.15 p.m.
Simple Simon and Friends
21, 23, 24, 26, 27, 28 Dec.;
2, 3, 4 Jan.
BOOK NOW

w/c December 15th.
YAKITY YAK
w/c December 22nd.
BERNIE CLIFTON
w/c December 29th.
"VIVA LAS VEGAS"
STUART GILLIES
BERNIE CLIFTON
This show is direct from the "WATERSPLASH" in Jersey.
w/c January 5th.
O'HARA'S PLAYBOYS

AQUARIUS NIGHT CLUB, Sheffield Road, Chesterfield. Tel: 70188/9

Peter Gordeno meets Sheila Cupit (was Sheila Tonks)

Sue Baker: *"Saw Bernard Manning. And Freddie Star. Amongst others."*

line-up. They all turned up dressed for dinner and I always remember the head Rotarian coming backstage asking if he could have a word with Mr Manning. And I said, 'Yes, no problem'.

"Bernard said, 'Alright squire' and the Rotarian said, 'I hope you don't mind me mentioning this but we have our ladies with us this evening and we would be so grateful if you would tone your act to suit the company that's out there. And

Susan Pope: *"Aquarius Night Club was brilliant, they had some really good acts one of the funniest was Cannon and Ball, I have so many memories of the nights I spent there, always remember their scampi in a basket."*

Linda Biggs: *"Maxi dresses, platform shoes, Moussec, dancing on the tables to Edwin Starr, basket meals, George Nafhu. Then there were the great hen nights, work outings, birthday and anniversary parties. Fond memories of close friends and colleagues, the songs of the time, and meeting countless celebrities."*

Bernard said, 'Don't worry pal, done a lot of these. It'll be fine'.

"Well to say that to Bernard was like a red rag to a bull. He went out and his first gag went along the lines of , '...Well he's giving her one and he's giving her one good. And she said, 'Just a minute, before you carry on, don't you think you should take precautions?' And he said, 'I have done, I've tied a plank across mi arse'.

"Within ten minutes he'd emptied the club. He absolutely went for their throats. Talk about the wrong place at the wrong time for the rotarians.

"I got away with my life that night."

"Probably the one aspect of my tenure there were the presentations. They started to become a kind of a cult thing.

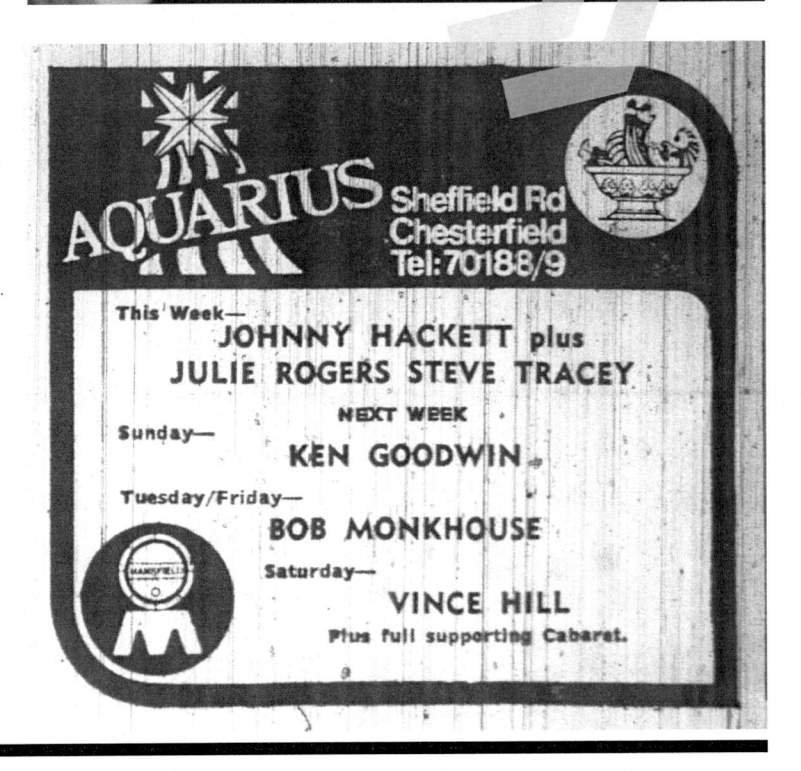

AQUARIUS Sheffield Rd, Chesterfield Tel: 70188/9

This Week—
JOHNNY HACKETT plus
JULIE ROGERS STEVE TRACEY
Sunday—
NEXT WEEK
KEN GOODWIN
Tuesday/Friday—
BOB MONKHOUSE
Saturday—
VINCE HILL
Plus full supporting Cabaret.

Dirty Stop Outs Guide to 1980s Chesterfield — **AQUARIUS** Edition

16

Club regulars

Below: The Aquarius was Club Mirror's 'Club of the Year' in 1979 – which members of staff do you recognise from that triumphant era?

Kate Caulfield: "My hen night 1973 - fell over and bumped my head in the loo - spent all my lunch break next day getting the right eye shadow combination to match my black:blue eye - great night."

The first half of the evening would be support acts and then a long interval - maybe an hour. And then you'd start the presentations and you'd end up with probably half a dozen hen parties coming in. The prospective bride would be dragged up on stage and then all these obscene items would come out of a box. There'd be champagne, drinks, flowers, photographs being taken by Gerald the photographer.

"The Aquarius was the place to come and celebrate.

"I always felt sorry for the main acts of the evening because of instead of going on at midnight they be wondering if these presentations would ever finish.

> "Then there was Big George - he was a former boxer, man mountain and no one ever saw him physically throw anyone out. He was about six foot four."

"Then there was Big George - he was a former boxer, man mountain and no one ever saw him physically throw anyone out. He was about six foot four. He never needed to exert any physical violence as his presence was enough. He had a team that would take no prisoners but Big George was again, a big feature of the venue.

"At that time it was like a pyramid of entertainment for acts. There was a vast number of Working Men's Clubs where you'd get to practice your act, then you'd got the cabaret clubs where acts would have the chance of being seen by TV producers.

AQUARIUS Sheffield Rd Chesterfield Tel: 70188/9

Thursday and Friday:
BOB MONKHOUSE
Saturday, 14th to 28th July
VINCE HILL
STU FRANCIS
From the Comedians
IVOR WYNNE and JENNY
Compere: Birni Clifton

Marilyn Thomas: "Worked there for seven years when it first opened, loved every minute of it. Pity the cabaret scene ended."

They were great days and it just won't happen again."

Few names were more synonymous with the Aquarius than compere Tufty Gordon.

Entertainment was in his DNA. Sheffield born, he began playing the saxophone at 14 and became equally proficient at the clarinet, flute, oboe and piccolo. He became a session musician and worked with artists spanning Tony Christie to Joe Cocker.

He even went on to compère at the first snooker championships at the Crucible.

Ian Jones: "Tufty was an absolute pro. Everything revolved around him on stage at the Aquarius. He seemed inexhaustible. He was without a doubt one of the most gifted entertainers you'd ever find."

Sue John: "I'm flooded by memories of a childhood spent in the Aquarius club... Yes a childhood. It was the mid '70s and a was 15. We never got asked for proof of age. My best friend at school (Hollingwood Girls school) Carole Bowler had an older sister, Pauline, and we formed a friendship and a love of the Aquarius. Pauline would walk from her house in Hollingwood to my parents in Rother Avenue, Brimington, and we would walk from there to the club. I would only have a pound or so in my purse but knew I had enough for a couple of lagers and black. My 16th birthday was spent in the cabaret lounge. It was either scampi and chips or chicken and chips in a plastic basket... luxury.

"The club was so fab as there were people of all ages. The early part of the evening in the nightclub was younger people and then once the cabaret had finished the older people would flood into the nightclub. I remember dancing the night away to 'Heaven Must Be Missing An Angel'. Although very young, I never felt vulnerable or at risk, it was a very different time. I was there New Year's Eve of 1976 and remember lads forming an orderly queue to give me a New Year's Kiss.

"The club and cabaret room felt really sophisticated and almost cosmopolitan as there were people there from all over Derbyshire and Yorkshire. I have spent all my adult life living and working in Birmingham, the West Midlands and London and I travel extensively with a home in Dubai but my childhood Saturday nights will never be beaten. I have the Aquarius to thank for such powerful memories."

Dirty Stop Outs Guide to **1980s** Chesterfield **AQUARIUS** Edition

The Aquarius in full swing in the 1970s

DIRTY STOP OUTS' GUIDE TO 1980s CHESTERFIELD

THOMPSON TWINS TO THE RESCUE

CHAPTER TWO

The luxury of Joplins wine bar

Vinyl (there was also the cassette but it never held the cultural status of the 7 inch single or album) was the one form of affordable escapism left to your average '80s dole-ite as they counted down the days to the expected Cold War-charged Armageddon.

Chesterfield was literally brimming with record shops where you could lose yourself for an entire afternoon amongst the hallowed racks of vinyl sleeves.

First and foremost was Connection which was dark, cool and independent; this was punk and indie heaven with metal and a few other genres thrown in for good measure.

And not forgetting the second hand section down the middle of the shop and the odd sale where they'd throw open the upstairs (though this occurrence was very rare).

More mainstream - well they'd spent more on lighting at least which helped open it up to all ages - was Hudsons. This was a shop that kept the town furnished in sounds (both vinyl, cassette and the ability to make your own music via their musical instrument shop) for decades, they even had an outlet in the Market Hall which added yet another stop off point for your afternoon crawl around all things music.

In the pre-download era, everyone from Woolworths to Boots to Littlewoods boasted a record section and your vinyl collection was a true measure of your worth - well that and the amount of Sounds and NMEs you had. There was also the renowned Startrak in the Shambles area.

Andrew Short said: "A Saturday afternoon trawl round the town centre was an absolute given in the 1980s. I don't think I missed one, ever. The only break you'd have was a coffee in Joplin's or Littlewoods. We'd regularly visit the same record shop two or three times in an afternoon. It seemed quite a normal thing to do."

Chesterfield, much to the excitement of many, was the epicentre of mainstream charts in the mid-1980s thanks to the Thompson Twins - a band with

DIRTY STOP OUTS' GUIDE TO 1980s CHESTERFIELD

strong links to the town.

Hits like 'Doctor! Doctor!' and 'Hold Me Now' were common currency on most dance floors in the region.

But there was little doubt the era's charts belonged to the Human League from nearby Sheffield; it was their sound and image that helped

ADAM & EVE
LORDSMILL STREET, CHESTERFIELD. TEL: 78834

SPRING FLING
MONDAYS
OVER 14's DISCO
ADMISSION 50p
7.00p.m.-10.00p.m.
MONDAYS
OVER 18's DISCO
FREE ADMISSION 10.00p.m.-2.00a.m.
PLUS 55p DRINKS PER NORMAL MEASURE
TUESDAY
NURSES' PARTY NIGHT
ADMISSION £1
PLUS 55p DRINKS PER NORMAL MEASURE
TUESDAY, 15th MAY
PYJAMA PARTY
PLUS 55p DRINKS PER NORMAL MEASURE
WEDNESDAY, 16th MAY
DIG THIS DRILL
THURSDAY
HEN PARTY NIGHTS
PLUS 55p DRINKS PER NORMAL MEASURE
FRIDAY
SUPER SCENE
SATURDAY WEEKEND PARTY NIGHT
CALLING ALL DOCTORS AND NURSES
MONDAY TO THURSDAY
ADMISSION FREE
LADIES
PASSES AVAILABLE FREE
THURSDAY, FRIDAY AND SATURDAY
COME AND ENTER OUR SPRING FLING

define the look for many in the town as Phil Oakey-style asymmetric haircuts became more and more popular.

The all-conquering synth act helped open the floodgates for the city's electro-pop movement.

The influence of the Human League's 1981 triple platinum 'Dare' album and multi-million selling 'Don't You Want Me' still resonates as strong today as it did as when it was first released.

Their sound was everywhere in Chesterfield - school discos, youth clubs, supermarkets, nightclubs, over the airwaves. The band broke Europe and the States. The world was at their feet.

But the Human League were only half of the Sheffield sound that was gaining airplay at the time

Heaven 17, formed out of the remains of the first incarnation of the band, were also massive.

The trio formed by former Oakey sidekicks Martyn Ware and Ian Craig Marsh together with vocalist Glenn Gregory also enjoyed chart success for the majority of the era.

Named after a fictional band in cult film 'A Clockwork Orange', they were politically astute, cool and gave a further dimension to the city's influence on the country's music and fashion scene.

Their biggest single of the era was 'Temptation' which reached number 2 in the UK singles chart in 1983 but a raft of other hits like '(We Don't Need This) Fascist Groove Thing', 'Come Live With Me' and 'Crushed By The Wheels Of Industry' keep them in demand to this day.

Glossy and witty, ABC were formed out of the ashes of Vice Versa. The band successfully prised no less than four hit singles from debut album 'The Lexicon Of Love'.

They made their debut at Sheffield's Psalter Lane Art College in September 1980. The audience were pretty gobsmacked by the band's total transformation from arty alternative to American funk with the image to go with it.

It was a meteoric and well choreographed rise to the top. They were signed within months and in the top twenty with 'Tears Are Not Enough' by November 1981.

It's fair to say that 1982 belonged to ABC. They shot down their cynics and eclipsed their rivals with three massive top ten hits that are still played on the radio as much as they ever were: 'Poison Arrow', 'The Look Of Love' and 'All Of My Heart'.

The subsequent album, 'The Lexicon Of Love', was a huge hit both here and in the States and stayed on the UK charts for a year. Their gold lamé suits became synonymous with eighties style and excess.

Though still years away from bothering the commercial charts, Jarvis Cocker's Pulp beavered away through the era with numerous line-up changes, numerous gigs and one extended stay in hospital.

The enigmatic front man had decided to try and impress a girl with his Spiderman impression and managed to fall out of a first-floor flat window.

"It was senseless bravado", he quipped. "Which is quite out of character. I realised I didn't have the strength to do it, or to climb back in, so I had to count to three and let go."

He didn't stop a few injuries stop him from performing - he gigged in a wheelchair.

The band played a well remembered gig at Chesterfield College in the late 1980s.

Bland frontman Rat

DIRTY STOP OUTS' GUIDE TO 1980s CHESTERFIELD

◀ No better time to be a teenager

Carl Flint said: "It was a time of great energy in Chesterfield, for a local teenager at that time Chesterfield seemed to be the centre of the universe. There were lots of bands, pubs, and fanzines - why would anyone ever want to leave?

"It was an exciting, if oppressive, time in the UK. A common hatred of Thatcher brought a lot of people together. Opposition to the Conservative government and their policies was a creative catalyst for a lot of young people. Suddenly there was a lot going on. CND was still around, as was Rock Against Racism, then there was Artists Against Apartheid, the miners' strike and lots of other stuff.

"I spent a lot of time at '48' drop-in centre - mostly making badges for young mods (there was a mini mod revival going on at the time), I really liked that badge machine - there was something very satisfying about using it - a design classic. I also contributed bits and pieces to the 48-based fanzine Hope.

"I miss the bands, the pubs, the fanzines, the people and the energy, but most of all I miss my youth.
"Kraftwerk at Sheffield City Hall, Chapter 2's farewell gig at Chesterfield Goldwell Rooms. Lots of things at the Leadmill. Redskins were good, can't remember where I saw them though. I went to loads of local Chesterfield gigs but they've all faded through time into one distant, drunken blur.

"Billy Bragg played at the Goldwell Rooms, I must have been there - I've seen photos.

"The best club by far was the Fusion on Thursday nights - even when that strange guy with the centre parting and medallion was DJing it was still better than anywhere else in the area.

"We used to go to the Adam & Eve on Monday nights, they had a sort of indie/futurist/alternative night. Not a great club though - horrible bouncers, horrible carpets.

"The Buck was a very popular pub, we used to go there a lot, I think it was the main 'alternative' hang out, especially on Fusion night. It's Carter's Bar or something like that now, isn't it?

"We also used to go to the Civic/Pomegranate - it was mostly fine! White Swan (Mucky Duck...zzzz) was okay too, mostly punky gigs I think. We also used to go to the Trap 7 bar upstairs at the Hare & Greyhound, it was also a live venue. A very small live venue.

"New club nights were also starting up around the time I left Chesterfield to go to art college in Leeds - Gotham City and later Polka Dot at Fascination, I think there were others too. I didn't get to many of either of those as I was no longer local.

"Well, I still like baggy suits and long overcoats, but I wouldn't call them an outrageous fashion statement. I had a pair of suede pointy boots that were too tight and pointy to walk in so I had to change into them when I got to Fusion and then change back into trainers when it was time to take the long walk home back to North Wingfield - the last bus home was around midnight which is just when Fusion was getting warmed up. It was always a tough choice to decide 'Should I stay or should I go?' when midnight was looming. It's no fun though walking back all that way at two or three in the morning, especially when you've got to get up for school the next day."

Making their indelible mark in the eighties

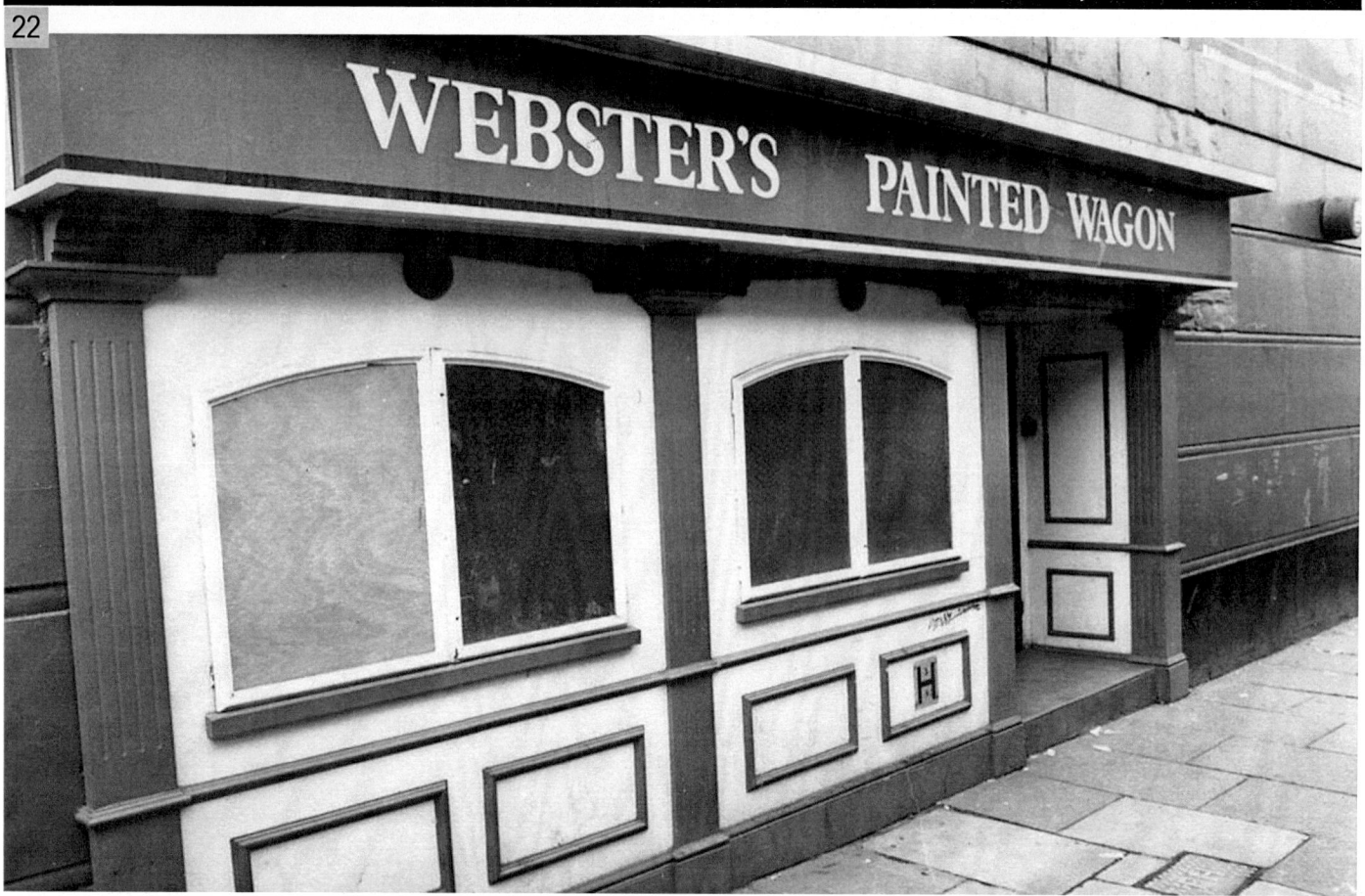

Dirty Stop Outs Guide to **1980s Chesterfield** **AQUARIUS** Edition

Above: The infamous Painted Wagon

Spires

Painted Wagon gets a Spires-style makeover

Gerry Kilmore was at the helm of Spires – the sprawling bar that fed the Aquarius nightclub weekend after the weekend.

The venue had been shown a clean pair of heels since its transformation from its former Painted Wagon guides.

It had glitz, it had fun pub feel and it even boasted a dancefloor.

"I have so many fond memories of the place", said Gerry Kilmore. "There was a real buzz about the place. It always had a bit of reputation as the Painted Wagon, but I put down a dance floor and it changed. Don't get me wrong we always had a fight or two but it was handled very quickly with really good doormen.

"We were always the first and last port of call I remember thinking when I went outside - if I put my watch to 8pm and 10 pm it was like watching a herd of buffalo coming down Cavendish St from every direction

"A very funny memory was when PC Davenport was on patrol one Xmas eve with another officer stopped outside the Spires and asked if we was busy I stood in the doorway so he couldn't get past me and I said oh we have only about Fifty in I would have lost my License - we had 900 plus in think my capacity was 350."

Many of the nightclubs fed off the busy Spires. Gerry Kilmore admits the venue would never have had the success it did without a very strong team around it

He said: "Here's a few names I would like to mention - Liam O Sullivan, Nick Jones, Dudley Annible, Jon Miller, Julia Carlisle, Sara and Darren Burton, Mandy and Anita Jones, Fred Quayle, Mark Wilcockson, Lisa Calladine, Carl Miles, Eddie McDermott, Vic Jarvis, Pete Brown, Mark Naylor and Mick Greaves. And to some fond memories of John Williamson the Aquarius owner."

DIRTY STOP OUTS' GUIDE TO 1980s CHESTERFIELD

23

Photobooth photography was the way forward in the pre-mobile world

It wasn't unusual for suburban pubs to look more like someone's front room in the era - here's the Bridge Inn

The original line-up of local rockers Stateline

◀"The best club by far was the Fusion on Thursday nights - even when that strange guy with the centre parting and medallion was DJing it was still better than anywhere else in the area."

Looking mysterious wasn't uncommon in the '80s

DIRTY STOP OUTS' GUIDE TO 1980s CHESTERFIELD

Motorhead drummer Phil 'Animal' Taylor (right) who originated from Hasland with Saxon (and later Motorhead) drummer Pete Gill

The all-conquering Human League

Sheffield's own Vice Versa, shortly before becoming ABC

Jerry Dammers of the Specials - the band played at Chesterfield's Fusion in their early days

Clare Grogan of chart stars Altered Images

DIRTY STOP OUTS' GUIDE TO 1980s CHESTERFIELD

'VIDEO NASTIES' FROM CHESTERFIELD CO-OP

CHAPTER THREE

The Co-op - where you could hire your video nasties

Society's do-gooders had a true field day with the emergence of the 'video nasty' - a group of low budget, generally crap horror films that avoided censorship by being distributed for purely video screening at home.

The term was first coined in 1982 and the films, demonised by commentators such as Mary Whitehouse, were soon said to be threatening the very fabric of society.

The films, especially the ones eventually banned, became the 'must see' items for any self-assuming teenager of the decade.

Video rental shops seemed to spring up anywhere and everywhere as the country struggled to decide which playback system to adopt: Betamax, Philips Video 2000 or the eventual winner, VHS.

With 'video nasties' available to rent anywhere from backstreet newsagents to Co-op electricals in Chesterfield town centre, an all-night, televised orgy of horror/violence was a must for all teenagers of the era.

It was the wedding of Charles and Diana in 1981 that was seen as the turning point for video cassette recorders.

Their big day was seen as the cause for a 50% increase in the number of people owning one.

A year later one in five households had one.

There was confusion initially as to how to censor this new style of home movie screening but, following the emergence of these shockers and column inches afforded to them by the likes of the Daily Mail, the lack of regulation didn't remain for long.

One of the biggest fears was the change of ways the viewer could consume the content.

In cinemas the film was simply screened - end of. At home, armed with a video cassette player, you could freeze frame, play in slow-motion, and wallow in on-screen violence for days at a time.

Oh and there was also the chance the minors might stick on the likes of 'I Spit On Your Grave', probably the most notorious of the 'video nasty' genre, whilst you were busy cooking the tea in the next room.

DirtyStopOuts.COM

DIRTY STOP OUTS' GUIDE TO 1980s CHESTERFIELD

The Daily Mail, unsurprisingly, led the charge for the censorship with its rabble-rousing words: 'RAPE OF OUR CHILDREN'S MINDS'.

It said: "The whole instinct of this newspaper is against regulation and restriction. But on the issue of video nasties we have no doubt whatsoever that regulation and restriction is the only answer."

The 1984 Video Recordings Act was duly passed and a (very) long list of prohibited films published.

Video nasty hits (before they were banned at least) included: 'The Evil Dead', 'Zombie Flesh Eaters', 'Driller Killer', 'The Killer Nun', 'The Burning', 'Island of Death', 'Cannibal Apocalypse' and 'Last House On The Left'.

Tom Stephen said: "I remember we watched 'The Burning' over and over for a whole night. I can't remember if it was already banned at that point or we were watching it pre-banning order. Whatever it was, we knew we were watching the hottest and most horrific film around and we bragged about it to everyone.

"I remember watching it on Halloween about ten years ago. It was absolutely crap and not scary at all. I think the whole 'video nasty' tag was a brilliant marketing wheeze dreamt up to promote crap horror - it was genius!"

Whilst Sheffield City Council funded free gigs to keep their unemployed happy in the early eighties, Chesterfield's ABC hit back with horror.

It was around 1984 that they used to promote Friday morning horror double bills for next to nothing to keep the doleites off the streets. At least it got us up in a morning.

Tom Stephen said: "I think you just showed your UB40 and you got a double-bill of horror every Friday morning for free. Today's unemployed don't seem to get the concessions we used to in the 1980s."

Queens Park

The Gardeners Arms - a must for many a weekend pub crawl

Appearance was everything - even for occasional goths

DIRTY STOP OUTS' GUIDE TO 1980s CHESTERFIELD

IN THE MOOD
CLOTHES OF YESTERYEAR
1920-1960's FASHIONS

GRANDAD SHIRTS
MALE + FEMALE SUITS
COATS
LACE + SILK BLOUSES
SUITS
JEWELLERY
BAGS
SHOES
AND MUCH MORE!!
ALL ORIGINALS
119 SALTERGATE, CHESTERFIELD (near football ground)

The Railway

◀Fiona Scroggs sums up her era: "Joplins, Live Aid gig at the Bradbury club with Screaming Lord Sutch!! Everyone used to have their hair cut at Mr Mopps where the trainees worked, I think (above Just Hair). We used to buy clothes from Frock Horror in Sheffield and then on a Saturday parade about in front of Woolworths like freaks! Not forgetting Jeanery and Mainstop in the precinct and Roosters on Chatsworth Road, the first diner in Chessy!"

Collecting for the Hillsborough Disaster of 1989

Brampton's St Thomas' Church entertained a wedding with a difference in the era

DIRTY STOP OUTS' GUIDE TO 1980s CHESTERFIELD

Thousands gather for the arrival of Charles and Diana in 1981

Cricket in Queen's Park

DIRTY STOP OUTS' GUIDE TO 1980s CHESTERFIELD

Life was a beach

Art college characters

The Dolebusters gigs in Sheffield's Weston Park attracted many from Chesterfield

Youth styles were as varied as the wallpaper in the era

Fusion promoter & Connection main man Stuart

DIRTY STOP OUTS' GUIDE TO 1980s CHESTERFIELD

Derby Road viaduct at Horns Bridge prior to demolition

Bingo was still in big demand

DIRTY STOP OUTS' GUIDE TO 1980s CHESTERFIELD

MULLETS AND MORE FOR THE MASSES

CHAPTER FOUR

The Barley Mow

Hair was everything in the 1980s and the more of it the better as far as most people were concerned.

Styles reached almost mythical heights thanks to crimpers, Insette hairspray, soap, scrunch drying, sugar and water and every other wild and wonderful method employed to keep bouffants airborne.

If that didn't create the shock value required there was always the option of dousing it in dayglo 'Crazy Colour' (or later 'Directions') - a guaranteed head turner and the very real added opportunity of getting the shit kicked out of you depending of what bar or club you happened to be walking past.

Whether you were sporting a towering mohawk, a Phil Oakey-led asymmetric, a backcombed gothic rat's nest, a U2-style mullet or you felt more at ease with a big breezy scrunched dried Sharon and Tracy-style bouffant, this was the era that welcomed every possible permutation of hirsute disaster with open arms.

Going bald was not really an option in the eighties (unless you were a skinhead of course). And if you did, there was always the option of a Scargill-style comb-over, a style that was still very much in vogue and virtually

DIRTY STOP OUTS' GUIDE TO 1980s CHESTERFIELD

acceptable at the time but it was advisable to be over 30.

It's not really surprising hair was big in the era - it was decade defined by the gargantuan and the pumped up bodies of Stallone and Schwarzenegger.

Whatever you might have heard in the press, size really did matter in the 1980s.

Cinemas were reborn as sprawling Multiplex's; supermarkets became football-stadium-like superstores and once busy shopping streets were left for dead by a new breed of out-of-town shopping centres.

Whilst most were happy with just one hairstyle, the era even gave rise to '2 in 1'. There was nothing more representative of this fine eighties trait than the humble mullet - strictly business out front and party land at the back.

Hair central in Chesterfield was definitely the Anchor - hangout for the rockers and the eighties breed of 'hair metal' led by the likes of Def Leppard and others.

The bar did more than its bit to populate the likes of nearby rock clubs like Rebels in Sheffield and Rock City in Nottingham. The best Chesterfield had was 'rock night' at the nearby Adam & Eve on a weekday.

So who was actually to blame for these car crash fashions that found their way to the streets of Chesterfield and right across the land?

Few have more to answer for than the 'Material Girl' herself, Madonna.

Her look was mirrored right across the country: Pink, dyed hair; torn stockings; bangles and crosses everywhere, big crimped hair and string vest.

Her layered look defined much of the era for females. Virtually every girl (even if they didn't admit it at the time) wanted the Madonna-look. Some were more successful than others.

Closer to home there was always the sassy look of Clare Grogan of Altered Images - another female icon.

For men (and regularly women to be honest) there was no one more dashing and influential than Mr Adam Ant.

His swashbuckling, post-punk music and fashion was just the kind of escapism required in a era defining by turmoil.

His movement was very much elegance and decadence all rolled into one - his trailblazing cartoonish image of pirates, Western men and Native Americans was evident throughout the era in a number of youth fashion genres.

Many eighties fashions deserve to stay in that era never to return. Others have fought valiantly to live on or make a comeback.

Leggings are now fully integrated back into mainstream society. Skin-tight jeans thankfully are not and neither are stonewash denims.

Other items still on the fashion scrapheap that were de rigueur in the 1980s include body suits, leg warmers, rah-rah skirts, 'FRANKIE SAYS RELAX' shirts and baggy mohair jumpers.

Other fashions and fashion observations of the era include...

Kim Miles said: "Crimped hair?"

David Malf Palfreyman said: "Donkey jacket."

Roland Gent said: "A massive quiff."

Kris Kneller said:
"Beer down ya 'Pogues t.shirt..."

Nicola Heathcote-Hems said: "Shoes from Rebina."

Androo Wobble said:
"Big hair and when I say big I mean massive and when I say massive I mean er well whatever... hairspray hung heavy in the air in Gotham City."

Carl Flint said:
"Gotham City - 50% hair/50% people."

Shaun Dale Ashmore said:
"Jacket sleeves pushed up like Don Johnson!"

Ian Smith said:
"Trousers from Hot legs? ' Spencer' pleats n Bowie bags. An yes, granddad cardigan amongst other clothing in burgundy, grey, black, white? Rebina shoes n clobber or mail order Phaze or Melanddi. Which of the handful of record shops did we go to get the latest vinyl esp 12" ltd editions?? Pirate boots, leg warmers, fingerless gloves, white placket shirts, King Kurt / Paul King hi-rise flat-top quiffs, or a broad mohican."

Mick Taylor said:
"Italian combat jackets German para boots."

DIRTY STOP OUTS' GUIDE TO 1980s CHESTERFIELD

The interior of Bejeranos

◀Paul Smith said: "I remember queuing in the foyer of the Adam & Eve one night. A bloke staggered in after me and fell over, he was absolutely paralytic. Two bouncers rushed out with the urgency of paramedics on a life or death mission; they picked him up, rushed him to the front of the queue and helped him to the pay desk. They helped him to get his money and then proceeded to walk him into the club and sat him on a stool at the bar and helped him purchase a drink. You don't get service like that these days."

Saltergate's County Hotel

DIRTY STOP OUTS' GUIDE TO 1980s CHESTERFIELD

◀Highlights of the nitespots

It's easy to forget the massive cultural changes that have taken place in recent years in terms of nightlife.

It's rare you'd be out prior to 9pm these days, safe in the knowledge there'll be bars open to the small hours. If you fancy a dance there'll be clubs serving alcohol later still.

The 1980s were very different. Things were far more stringent. Pubs shut at 11pm, nightclubs at 2am. No ifs, no buts - arguments normally meant rough justice doled out by even rougher bouncers.

Chesterfield's Aquarius had developed from its cabaret routes to be the mainstream nightclub of the era. Hundreds made the journey from the town centre every Friday and Saturday night.

The double decker buses that used to line up outside the Painted Wagon (and later Spires as it became known) were absolute bedlam on the way down.

Dress codes at the venue were stringent. It was always amusing to see dressed down punks trying their damndest to look at ease in a collar and jacket.

If you got in early you might catch the end of the cabaret act in the back room (they had some pretty major acts) - the main event used to take place at the various areas at the front of the venue.

It was a big club that used to attract audiences from right around the region.

The Aquarius was a mainstream club through and through. If any non-trendy fancied drinking past 11pm in the 1980s on a weekend they needed to dress accordingly.

The alternative types were demoted to weekday clubbing at the likes of Fusion (at the start of the era before it shutdown), Fascination and the Adam & Eve.

Vying for the Aquarius's weekend crowd later in the era was new kid on the block, the Moulin Rouge.

They'd got a big advantage over 'the Acka' - they were town centre based and within spitting distance of feeder pubs like the Blue Bell and others.

It was a big hit for much of the era.

But it's fair to say the Aquarius held its own for the majority of the decade, hitting back with its madly popular 'over 25s' Thursday night.

If all else failed there was always the Adam & Eve on Lordsmill Street. Rather less biblical than its name inferred, it generally went where other venues feared to tread.

Paul Smith said: "I remember queuing in the foyer of the Adam & Eve one night. A bloke staggered in after me and fell over, he was absolutely paralytic. Two bouncers rushed out with the urgency of paramedics on a life or death mission; they picked him up, rushed him to the front of the queue and helped him to the pay desk. They helped him to get his money and then proceeded to walk him into the club and sat him on a stool at the bar and helped him purchase a drink. You don't get service like that these days."

Last but not least was Fascination (later to become Montmartre), the small, underground venue which became renowned for its mid-week, cut price lager nights which became an even bigger reason for the town's unemployed never to get a job.

DIRTY STOP OUTS' GUIDE TO 1980s CHESTERFIELD

Anchor regulars

Less is more - the Miss Glam Rock competition held at Sheffield's Roxy's was a big hit

DIRTY STOP OUTS' GUIDE TO 1980s CHESTERFIELD

The Lord Nelson - hangout for pensioners, punks and winos

The Star on Chatsworth Road

Red Lion landlord Peter Bates (second from left) in party mood

DIRTY STOP OUTS' GUIDE TO 1980s CHESTERFIELD

LIVE AID COMES TO TOWN

CHAPTER FIVE

Though the buildings have passed the test of time, the fashions have not...

The honour of uniting the country and taking its mind of impending nuclear war, the Miners' Strike and mass unemployment fell to one man (or at least he decided it should be his job) - Bob Geldof.

His Band Aid/Live Aid movement was a stroke of genius - not bad for a man who was falling off the radar thanks to the floundering career of his Boomtown Rats, who'd enjoyed massive success just a few years earlier.

Seen by many as the defining moment for music in the era, it started in 1984 with the Christmas number one, 'Do They Know It's Christmas?' - a song penned by Bob Geldof and Ultravox's Midge Ure.

Though a pretty appalling tune by anyone's standards, it went on to sell millions and, as Bob Geldof pointed out many times: "This is not just any record. It is a way of helping to stop people from dying" - give him his dues, he could always be relied to knock out a good sound bite when required.

Few people would have been capable of pulling together the galaxy of stars that sang on the disc. The Band Aid super group was a true who's who of pop circa 1984.

Everyone from U2 to Duran Duran turned up to the Notting Hill recording studio to be a part of the single.

Its success also helped spawn a clutch of spin-off releases spanning 'We Are The World' by USA For Africa in the USA to 'Hear 'n' Aid' by various metal artists.

But not everyone was in support of the move. Morrissey wasn't slow in coming forward

DIRTY STOP OUTS .COM

DIRTY STOP OUTS' GUIDE TO 1980s CHESTERFIELD

with his take on things.

He said at the time: "I'm not afraid to say that I think Band Aid was diabolical. Or to say that I think Bob Geldof is a nauseating character. Many people find that very unsettling, but I'll say it as loud as anyone wants me to. In the first instance the record itself was absolutely tuneless. One can have great concern for the people of Ethiopia, but it's another thing to inflict daily torture on the people of Great Britain. It was an awful record considering the mass of talent involved. And it wasn't done shyly it was the most self-righteous platform ever in the history of popular music."

But his outburst didn't stop the Live Aid movement from truly grabbing the attention of the country and much of the world.

Many who made the journey to Wembley Stadium said it was the best gig of their lives - there were 72,000 in attendance. An estimated 1.5 billion worldwide in 160 different countries were glued to the TV for the event's duration.

It was one of the biggest broadcasts in the history of the world. At one point in the day it was believed 95% of all TV sets on the planet were tuned in to the event.

The 16-hour music marathon also combined a simultaneous concert at JFK Stadium, Philadelphia in the States.

Bob Geldof frequently reminded viewers: "Don't go to the pub tonight. Please stay in and give us your money. There are people dying now."

Each artist, however iconic their status and gargantuan their ego, was given a maximum of 17 minutes to play. Songs were interspersed with films showing the famine in Africa the superstars were pledging to help.

The public reaction was unprecedented. Retailers recorded one of the worst days trading since records began and scores of towns and cities did their own version of Live Aid that summer.

At one point, the phone centre in the U.S. crashed when 700,000 pledge calls of cash for the appeal came in at the same time. By the end of the day in the States, more than $70 million had been raised.

Geldof earned himself a knighthood and swore that he would never attempt a sequel – a promise he broke when he staged Live 8 in 2005.

Andy Weatherton said: "It's true, the world really did seem to stop for Live Aid. We did go to the pub that night but we might as well not have bothered, the place was half empty."

Chesterfield, like many towns and cities across the country, had its own version at the Bradbury Club on Chatsworth Road. Scores of local artists performed for the cause.

Andy Weatherton said: "It was an event that truly brought people together, right down to a place like Chesterfield. Whatever your thoughts on Geldof, it was an incredible achievement."

DIRTY STOP OUTS' GUIDE TO 1980s CHESTERFIELD

◀Morrissey: "I'm not afraid to say that I think Band Aid was diabolical. Or to say that I think Bob Geldof is a nauseating character. Many people find that very unsettling, but I'll say it as loud as anyone wants me to. In the first instance the record itself was absolutely tuneless.

One can have great concern for the people of Ethiopia, but it's another thing to inflict daily torture on the people of Great Britain. It was an awful record considering the mass of talent involved. And it wasn't done shyly it was the most self-righteous platform ever in the history of popular music."

Chaos Bros

The Portakabins of Shepley's Yard - the cornerstone of the town's eighties retail offering

DIRTY STOP OUTS' GUIDE TO 1980s CHESTERFIELD

◀Dirty Mary or Talcy Malc?

Chesterfield had its fair share of 'characters' in the era. Many became came legendary - not always for the right reasons and you regularly have to ask where the 'care in the community' was at some points. Over two decades on and their names live on. Here's a few names you might remember...

Mark Adams said: "Lots of characters round town in them days. Buttercup, Dirty Mary, Talcy Malc, The Hatchet Man, brother and sister Ebb and Flo' from Boythorpe to name but a few.

Simon Popplewell said: "Dunc the Punk."

Steve Noz Norris said: "Just go to the Portland any day of the week... Same old pissheads... Same old people..."

Lorraine Alton said: "Apparently Buttercup got knocked down and killed years ago now. I can remember her outside the Adam & Eve. She threatened me with a dinner knife she got out of her suitcase, also in Clowne taking a pee under a bus shelter mid afternoon... Classy bird sadly missed lol.

"Dunc the Punk, definitely a character... Last memory of him was standing on a table in the cafeteria at college, preaching and waving his bible at us "sinners". Police were called and he was escorted off the premises..."

Linda Hickson said: "Dunc the Punk sent me a birthday cake through the post!!! I wouldn't eat it in case it was poisoned but my housemate did!"

Simon Popplewell said: "Through no fault of my own (landlord wouldn't give me my bond back because 'allegedly' his furniture was still smouldering outside) I ended up having to move into Dunc's house for a short while... Fook me that was interesting; first night I stayed I was coming back from somewhere and the fire brigade had arrived... Chip pan fire... They put the fire out, we stayed in the blackened and sooted house... I felt really safe :-/"

Simon Doherty said: "Vondra, pub singer from Whitt Moor with a beehive and a mini. She was 60 odd then."

Darrell Taylor said: "The guy in the brown suit that used to turn up to Adam & Eve rock night, drink halves and randomly drop to the floor and do press ups."

Mark Adams said: "Ebb n' Flo were a brother and sister of indeterminable age. They both had matted up birds nest like hair and were always together. Dirty Mary, also known as Black Mary, was a former Crown and Cushion beauty who would do owt for a half."

Androo Wobble said: "I had a drink with Buttercup in some old pub I cannot remember, she had style."

Andy Excess said: "She had something, probably several somethings ... ;)"

John Moules said: "Wow what flashbacks remembering all these people, they certainly brightened a night up with their antics. Smeg had a really bad bike accident which he only just survived, last I heard he'd become tee total and no longer sleeping on train tracks."

Richard Rodda said: "Some good memories of very strange people. I once twatted Nut in the Greyhound for taking the piss then regretted it after as I thought he was gonna come and find me when I wasn't so brave/drunk! Also what about Striker Lee Crow!"

Mark Davison said: "I remember Mary pissing herself at the bar and Webbo got hold of her to throw her out and she pissed on him too!!!"

DIRTY STOP OUTS' GUIDE TO 1980s CHESTERFIELD

◀Tufty Gordan to Johnny Crescendo

Simon Popplewell said: "Peter Bates wouldn't allow me in to his pub once just because I was in my school uniform. I walked outside, took tie & blazer off and put in my bag, walked straight back in & he served me a bottle of Newcy Brown... That was in 84. I was 13yrs old..... Happy days.... :)

"Johnny Crescendo (Alan Holdsworth), heard one of his old songs ('Choices and Rights') being played in the background on a BBC documentary about disability rights a few years ago. A few years further back I saw him on the news handcuffed to a bus, but no idea where he is now or what he's up to... Anyone know?"

Helen Hall said: "Tufty Gordon, old compere at the Aquarius night club. Those were the good old days, can we have them back please?"

Building the massive Pavements shopping centre with its centre-piece supermarket

Staff of Spires

Chesterfield Pitcher of the Year Bobby Halket in 1984

DIRTY STOP OUTS' GUIDE TO 1980s CHESTERFIELD

The Bluebell was a mainstay of mainstream bar entertainment throughout the era

Jim Spacey

DIRTY STOP OUTS' GUIDE TO 1980s CHESTERFIELD

ALTERNATIVE COMEDY AND A HOME FOR HENRY NORMAL

CHAPTER SIX

Queens Park Hotel - scene of much late night revelry towards the end of the era and beyond before being bulldozed itself

Few programmes had more influence over the youth of the 1980s than the anarchic 'Young Ones' that was first screened in 1982.

The show helped turn alternative comedy into mainstream entertainment and make massive stars of its cast and writers.

Rick (played by Rik Mayall) was the caricature of the kind of student everyone hated at the time - the middle-class undergraduate that chose to forget his upbringing for the duration of his degree, dress in charity shop clothes and spout politics he knew little or nothing about.

Then there was hapless hippy Neil (Nigel Planer). A total disaster area of a human being in all areas (and let's face it, everyone knew a Neil). Always depressed, always stoned and surviving on a diet of lentils.

Vyvyan (Adrian Edmonson) was a little more extreme - mostly at the expense of Rick and Neil who were regularly the victims of his random acts of violence. Though a supposed punk, you never quite got to the bottom of the reason for 'heavy metal' being emblazoned across his back in the days when the two youth cultures rarely mixed.

And then there was Mike (Christopher Ryan) - the supposed 'cool one'. A kind of Fonz with a difference, the Mike version had zero success with women.

In many ways the 'Young Ones' helped the media get a grip on youth culture in the

◀ *"Lowlights of the era were being beaten up in the grounds of the Crooked Spire and getting threatened by townies at the Civic."*

Dirty Stop Outs .COM

DIRTY STOP OUTS' GUIDE TO 1980s CHESTERFIELD

early eighties and pigeonhole the disparate groups.

It also made people realise so much of '80s fashion were reliant on throwbacks to previous eras.

The Teds of the 1950s were the basis of the rockabilly revival played out in the early 1980s with the likes of the Stray Cats, Matchbox, The Jets and other acts regularly bothering the charts.

There was also a massive '60s Mod revival led by the likes of The Jam, Secret Affair and the Merton Parkas.

Heavy metal had been banging around since around 1969 - we just had the New Wave of British Heavy Metal in the eighties to try and get things up to date and claw back ground lost to punk.

Though the 'Young Ones' was phenomenally popular it never had a chance of ranking alongside some of the most popular sitcoms of the era: the likes of 'Hi-De-Hi!', the 'Morecambe and Wise Show', 'Are You Being Served' and the 'Benny Hill Show'.

Thursday evenings, especially the early part, was non-negotiable for any self-assuming teenager - it was 'Top Of The Pops' that reigned supreme for the duration of the era.

One of the biggest televisional happenings of the 1980s was the launch of 'breakfast TV'. BBC and ITV unveiled their offerings almost simultaneously in 1983.

TV-AM was unveiled with massive fanfare in February. Early viewing figures were hugely disappointing, a stark contrast to the BBC's Breakfast Time which was seen as a big success with its easy magazine style.

Major in fighting at TV-AM together with the firing of presenters and general lack of direction saw ratings only start to improve with the installation of new presenters in the shape of Nick Owen and Anne Diamond and the unlikely pull of Roland Rat, a rodent puppet that became a massive hit with youngsters.

John Corker said: "I remember when Channel Four launched - we didn't get it for months. The only way we could occasionally see it was on our portable upstairs, the picture quality was a disgrace!

"Entertainment was governed by TV in the eighties. There seemed to be so many iconic moments that you were reliant on TV for. Boys From The Blackstuff shaped the mood of much of working class Britain in the early eighties and the aftermath of a nuclear holocaust was played out in its most shocking and horrific form in Threads."

Society's Victims

DIRTY STOP OUTS' GUIDE TO 1980s CHESTERFIELD

◀Comedian, and these days head of Steve Coogan's 'Baby Cow Productions', Henry Normal lived in Chesterfield in the 1980s. As well as his relentless gigging, he was one half of the partnership that set up Planet X Records in Newbold before it moved into the town centre. He was also the 'acceptable' face of Gotham City, the popular alternative night that ran at the Fascination nightclub.

Henry Normal said: "I was setting out on an adventure and I'd no idea where it would lead. I'd got some great mates with artistic careers which were burgeoning. It was an exciting time. You didn't know if anything was going to become of it but there was a great sense of optimism around.

"The romantic side of records shops is the fact you're dealing with vinyl and bands but in truth, you're just stood in a room for hours on end. And it was quite difficult to make a living at it - especially for two of us. I think even from the first month we opened it was destined not to last long.

"I was the doorman at Gotham City. Whenever someone was needed to talk to the management it was normally me as I wore a suit and was seen as the acceptable face of youth culture.

"I remember seeing Pulp, who I later toured with, and Dig V Drill at the Adam & Eve - not a club I'd ordinarily go to.

"I remember doing a gig at the college with the Body Factory.

"Steve Waterhouse was always a hero of mine - he personified a real way of living your life. He'd got a good sense of community, he'd got values and a grasp of politics. I used to pop down to his '48' place."

DIRTY STOP OUTS' GUIDE TO 1980s CHESTERFIELD

The only place to finish a night out - the Barbara Hepworth sculpture was rarely appreciated by the drunken revellers that used to end up in the makeshift paddling pool in front of the AGD building.

Dressed to kill

The march of progress outside Bryan Donkin works - another landmark that has since disappeared

DIRTY STOP OUTS' GUIDE TO 1980s CHESTERFIELD

◀ Synth was good, trendies not so good

Carl Flint said: "The emergence of synthesizer music was good for me - I never liked that long-haired, masturbatory guitar solo, denim clad rock music that seemed to have been around for so long, especially in this area. I liked new wave and punk but I was a bit too young to really 'get it' and I was too shy and quiet to be a punk as well. The detached cool of Kraftwerk, Human League and Cabaret Voltaire was the perfect soundtrack of my teenage life, because I was, like, so cool and detached.
"Lowlights of the era were being beaten up in the grounds of the Crooked Spire and getting threatened by townies at the Civic."

The Boythorpe - another trusty suburban hostelry of the era

◀ Lindsay McLaren said: "I thought Roland Rat was absolutely hilarious. It's bizarre how a puppet rat managed to single-handedly rescue an entire breakfast programme."

The building now better known as S41

DIRTY STOP OUTS' GUIDE TO 1980s CHESTERFIELD

The towering AGD building

Making the finishing touches to the outside of Boots prior to paving

Celebrating the town's heritage - dignitaries gather around the Market Place pump

The Shambles

DIRTY STOP OUTS' GUIDE TO 1980s CHESTERFIELD

THE BRAMPTON MILE - A TRUE RITE OF PASSAGE

CHAPTER SEVEN

The Three Horse Shoes under the watch of the great Fred Tipping complete with its legendary 'loony juice'

Few towns had an after dark induction assault course to match the legendary 'Brampton Mile'.

The toll of casualties over the years must stretch into the thousands as groups steered themselves to attempt a rite of passage rarely matched in the entire country at the time.

It started, in the 1980s at least, in the middle class surroundings of the Terminus Hotel (closed around 1999 and now demolished) - at least that was the start of our version of 'the mile', everyone seemed to have their own interpretation.

To have any chance of completing 'the mile' - and we're talking 11pm finish here in the '80s - you needed to have an early tea and be ready to rock around 5 to 5.30pm.

The Terminus had it easy. Though there was a sense of trepidation and excitement in the assembled masses, at least everyone was sober.

There was regularly a point to prove on the Brampton Mile.

The main one being the overriding ability to prove beyond reasonable doubt you could 'tek thi ale'.

At this particular point it wasn't an issue but it wasn't uncommon for certain characters to start with 'a pint' to really prove their worth. It would regularly be their undoing later.

The need for speed was an integral part of the Brampton Mile - '20 minutes a pub' was a figure etched in your brain (whilst it was still working at least).

Many people missed the Terminus altogether because of the length of time it took to get to the second pub, The Star; in

DIRTY STOP OUTS' GUIDE TO 1980s CHESTERFIELD

our eyes they're already fallen at the first hurdle.

We agreed, 'they're not true mile drinkers'.

The Star a was long and thin, sprightly hostelry well known for its popular mid-week quizzes.

The only question to be asked at this point on this night was pint, half or short?

There were a total of 18 pubs before the chequered flag was waved as you sank your last drink in the Square & Compass.

Even if you were drinking halves, that was still 9 pints, either that or 18 shorts. Anyone that could sink 18 pints in six hours and then take in a nightclub was a better man (or woman) than me. I'm sure it was completed by a few - whether they lived to tell the tale is questionable.

But you also have to remember that draught lager, on average, was less strong that it is today; its alcohol content stood at around 3% rather than the 4.5% to 5% you get today.

Getting from The Star to the Peacock was a few second jaunt. It wasn't much further to the next stop off either, down a backstreet.

At this point there wasn't the added time impediment of having to wait to be served. It was still early and regulars were still sobering up from Saturday dinnertime.

The Britannia and adjacent Rose & Crown were normally the first point of contact with non-mile drinkers. It was turned seven o'clock and the regulars were fast turning out - the gents regularly resplendently dressed in drain pipe jeans and white socks and the ladies in rah-rah skirts and white stilettos.

The next pub, the Three Horse Shoes, was regularly a crossroads for intrepid explorers.

Whilst the majority of the hostelries were deemed 'old men's pubs' (we were still years away from the 'The Brad' turning the whole area into Ches Vegas's answer to the Strip with discos in every bar), this place, run by the inimitable Fred Tipping, attracted a bizarre mix of pensioners, punks, rockers and goths.

The Three Horse Shoes boasted one great leveller - 'loony juice'. A vile, 8% strength cider that could regularly fell a man at a thousand paces (hence it was only ever served in halves).

The liquid seem to be responsible (or certainly blamed) for a multitude of sins: violence, adultery, larceny, getting arrested, being sick, kicking the living daylights out of the fruit machine at the back of the pub when it didn't pay out and keeling over being a few. The mere utterance of the words, 'he's been ont' loony juice', immediately confirmed you'd no control over your senses and the slate was wiped clean, whatever your sin.

Andrew Bannister said: "I remember the old man being like Mr Benn; we'd order some of the old loony juice, he'd disappear and re appear with two glasses of the cloudy stuff. Me and my mate David Moy got very drunk at the golden age of 15 !!!!"

Steve Waterhouse said: "Loony Juice... What an earth was in that? Chronic."

Fights regularly broke out in the

Another Brampton Mile watering hole on the way to the finishing post, the Royal Oak

DIRTY STOP OUTS' GUIDE TO 1980s CHESTERFIELD

Ye Olde Crooked Spire

'games area' - the space in the back of the pub that was home to the aforementioned fruit machine (and an antiquated, by today's standards and it didn't seemed that good in the eighties to be honest), video tank game.

Being 'banned from the Three Horse Shoes' for a spell wasn't that uncommon but it never normally lasted long - Fred was a much loved and forgiving soul.

Most mile drinkers had sense enough to give 'loony juice' a wide berth if they were going to have any chance of reaching the end.

Next off was the Prince of Wales, across the road. A rather more sedate place that didn't mix punks with pensioners - these days it's an up market French bar/eatery.

The next set of pubs was the Brampton Mile's answer to the Bermuda Triangle.

It was a trio of hostelries that would by now be very busy; they'd contain punters regularly itching for trouble and have landlords always on the look out for 'mile drinkers'.

Intrepid explorers were often now three or four hours into some pretty hectic drinking. The clock was ticking and there were already queues at the bars.

Splits would already be appearing in the ranks of larger parties. Someone wouldn't be paying their way, another would have been flagging and caught trying to hide their drink as to avoid getting in more of a state and another would be gearing up to demonstrating just how hard they were.

Landlords and landladies knew 'mile drinkers' were on a fight for survival at this point - one wrong move and their pride and joy could turn into a warzone. If they spotted revellers wavering between being unconscious and getting locked up for GBH they'd ring ahead to the next pub and warn them to be on their guard - or worse still, call the old Bill.

It wasn't uncommon for breakaway groups to throw in the towel altogether and dive on a bus into town whilst there was some semblance of order - there was a stop that sat between The Red Lion and the Barrel.

There was five minutes of respite if you survived. The next pub, though quite large, was the preserve of pensioners and it was more like entering someone's house

There was rarely any hassle in the New Inn or the nearby Grouse.

It wasn't too bad in the Alma either.

By now there was little chance of your party being in the same pub at the same time. You'd probably be spread out between two or three bars.

There'd now be at least one member of the party that would be totally annihilated and need holding up. One would invariably be covered in sick.

I must admit my first Brampton Mile attempt ended at the Grouse. I didn't feel ashamed, it was like the first time you make the jump in the first 'Matrix' film - 'no one makes it the first time'.

By my third attempt I knew my

◄ Andrew Bannister said: "I remember the old man being like Mr Benn; we'd order some of the old loony juice, he'd disappear and re appear with two glasses of the cloudy stuff. Me and my mate David Moy got very drunk at the golden age of 15 !!!!"

DIRTY STOP OUTS' GUIDE TO 1980s CHESTERFIELD

strategy; a vodka and orange in every pub. I sailed through it.

People will regularly complain that 'the Brampton Mile isn't like it was' and they'd be right. Even in the mid-1980s we were losing pubs and the pride that goes with necking a drink in 18 bars before you go clubbing.

We witnessed the end of the Bold Rodney as it was transformed into Ziggi's fun pub and then ended up as Dynasty Chinese restaurant.

The Square & Compass shut in later years moving the chequered flag back a pub to the Masons.

It was probably more a feeling of relief than that of elation as you sank the last drink. If you finished without attempting to knock seven bells out of another member of the party or catching your girlfriend snogging some random stranger you were truly a veteran mile man (or woman).

The Holy Grail for many mile drinkers - the sign outside the Square & Compass

DIRTY STOP OUTS' GUIDE TO 1980s CHESTERFIELD

Princess Di woos the crowd on her 1981 visit

Crowds gather for the Christmas lights

DIRTY STOP OUTS' GUIDE TO 1980s CHESTERFIELD

◀ Superhuman David McDermott gives his own interpretation of the epic 1980s pilgrimage. His expedition added a further three pubs to the total and completed it two hours quicker: "It was decided the mile started at the Terminus and included every one inside (the Britannia included) and the one that's now the Chinese. It finished at the Market, Sun and Portland inc and was to be done starting at 7pm and walking. You had to be done by closing time and still standing. I must admit I did not complete on every attempt."

DIRTY STOP OUTS' GUIDE TO 1980s CHESTERFIELD

Phoenix performing in New Square in 1983 for Chesterfield Smile Week

Morris Men (and women) in action

DIRTY STOP OUTS' GUIDE TO 1980s CHESTERFIELD

The Masons on Chatsworth Road, last pub bar one to the end of the Brampton Mile

Olde House Hotel general manager Thomas McHugh

Confirming your entry to the promised land

Fred Tipping (middle) and friends

DIRTY STOP OUTS' GUIDE TO 1980s CHESTERFIELD

FROM THE SPASMS TO THE SEPTIC PSYCHOS - TOWN'S OWN MUSIC HEROES

CHAPTER EIGHT

Prince of Wales on Chatsworth Road

Though no one reached the dizzy heights of the Thompson Twins trio (and the depths of their true local roots are debatable), there was no lack of productive spirit amongst the rest of the Chesterfield rock'n'roll massive in the era.

Our drive, enthusiasm and creative spirit was up there with any town or city in the UK, we just never got on 'Top Of The Pops' quite as many times... Or maybe it was we didn't want to - yeah, right?

Punk found a true working class soul mate in Chesterfield - especially when the second wave of the movement had come around in the early '80s and it was the green light for non-art students to get their working class teeth into things. The town truly got its rox off and then some to the era of leather, studs and acne.

The Fusion was the town's answer to Sheffield's legendary Limit - it played host to landmark gigs from everyone from the Specials to Punishment of Luxury before closing its doors for the last time in the early 1980s.

As far as locally produced carnage, the one that made arguably the biggest racket in terms of record sales was the Septic Psychos, led by brothers, Chiz and Mick Shakespeare.

They earned their inclusion on the national compilation album, 'Punk Dead - Nah Mate. The Smell Is Jus Summink In Yer Underpants Innit'. And the story doesn't start and finish in the eighties. They're probably bigger now than they ever were and regularly play throughout Europe, are regulars at

DIRTY STOP OUTS' GUIDE TO 1980s CHESTERFIELD

Blackpool's yearly Rebellion Festival and are chalking up new releases to the delight of an ever growing fan base.

Pez-led Criminal Sex were another firebrand of the era who left an indelible mark on the towns of Holland, their drummer Noz is still recovering.

Society's Victims were carnage personified.

The Spasms earned their stripes for their name alone but they were definately more '77 bred than '81. Needless to say they more than earned their place in the annals in Crooked Spire-charged music history.

The Corpse charged in whilst No Dead Meat trod a thin line between Chumbawamba-style equality and Chiz-charged red mist. There was also the Chaos Bros and the unforgettable night key members backed Screaming Lord Sutch at the White Swan.

As punk was dying it was left to skateboard chancers like Resurgence and The Distorted to fill the gaps in the Chesterfield rosters as the era battened down the hatches to wait out the Thatcher years.

Well that and the man that was, and continues to be, Chesterfield's answer to John Lydon (but arguably with far more creative spark when he lays off the cider), Rat.

The Bland front man took the post punk, phallic-imagery to new dimensions; in fact nearly out of Chesterfield.

Many cite Yah-Boo! as most likely to make it in the era. They had a lot going for them.

There were also other outfits like the Body Factory, Gah-Ga, Chapter 2, Passing Strangers, Jim Spacey, Dee & The Destitutes, Sanity Cabinet and Circus all vying for position on Gay Bolton's Derbyshire Times pop page and beyond.

In music terms there was only one way to avoid politics in the era - become a rocker.

There was no need to write anti-Thatcher diatribes anymore, your head had moved Stateside and the only thing you needed to worry about was replacing your Chesterfield drool with some glitzy LA twang (which wasn't always easy after eight cans of Red Stripe).

Few bands passed it off better than Spoilt Bratt with more than a nod to Motley Crue.

But there was plenty happening that owed more to the spirit of the British New Wave of British Heavy Metal with the likes of Saracen, Stateline, Roxberg and others.

Though Chesterfield was rarely (if at all) on Harvey Goldsmith's radar as he was planning out yet another money spinning UK tour, we did have

Sanity Cabinet

Dance floor action at the Adam & Eve

DIRTY STOP OUTS' GUIDE TO 1980s CHESTERFIELD

the odd event that caused the town to turn out on mass.

The era did play host to a few landmark visits by acts that would have previously given the town a wide berth: Pulp, Billy Bragg, the Membranes, the UK Subs, Flux of Pink Indians, Broken Bones and others.

Carl Flint said: "Local favourites of mine were Yah-Boo! and also Spasms/Chapter 2/Circus/Astronauts (have I missed any of their names out?).

"Yah-Boo! because they were so different from any of the other local bands around at the time. They seemed to have a different outlook as well as a different sound. For a while they seemed like the local band most likely to make it in the outside world (they didn't).*

"Chapter 2 because they had the best songs and the best singer. The songs still sound good today, most of their recordings were recently released on the CD 'Return of the Spud Gun Kids' - it's very good!

"I went to see lots of punk bands (Chaos Brothers, Criminal Sex, Footrot!) as well but the bands above stood out more because they weren't punk bands."

* True fact! As a teenager Ben Miles, actor in Coupling, V For Vendetta, etc, was a percussionist in Yah-Boo's original line-up.

There's still the odd mystery in terms of '80s Chesterfield. The main one being, who was the person that listed Bingo Reg and the Screaming Jeannies and Stuttering Jack and the Heart Attacks as performing at Chesterfield Top Rank?

The NME had them down as playing virtually every Saturday in the early part of the era and no bands of that name, as far as we know, ever played

Celebrations at the Moulin Rouge

A packed Moulin Rouge

Moulin Rouge DJ Nick Jones

DIRTY STOP OUTS' GUIDE TO 1980s CHESTERFIELD

◀Punk found a true working class soul mate in Chesterfield - especially when the second wave of the movement had come around in the early '80s and it was the green light for non-art students to get their working class teeth into things. The town truly got its rox off and then some to the era of leather, studs and acne.

The original Planet X shop in Newbold

Fashions took on many forms

DIRTY STOP OUTS' GUIDE TO 1980s CHESTERFIELD

The Pavements shopping precinct

Shepley's Yard

DIRTY STOP OUTS' GUIDE TO 1980s CHESTERFIELD

The completed Pavements Shopping Precinct

The derelict Peacock Inn that became the town's Tourist Information Centre for the majority of the era

DIRTY STOP OUTS' GUIDE TO 1980s CHESTERFIELD

HOME ENTERTAINMENT WAS THE STUFF OF NIGHTMARES FOR THE HAPLESS PARTY HOST

CHAPTER NINE ▶

The Sun

We might have been years off smart phones and social media but we didn't seem to need them where house parties were concerned.

Word of an impending event seemed to spread quicker than trending on Twitter.

Forget flash mobbing - house mobbing turned into a veritable after dark career for many in the era. In some cases the event could go on for two or three days as random strangers took over the running of the household.

The best house party potential was always those rumoured to be taking place in the more affluent parts of town and, even to this day, it's hard to imagine why an earth people entertained the idea of having such a thing on their own doorstep (well, it was normally the parents' house who would be away on holiday).

You could always tell when the 'host' was making their debut on the circuit; they'd invariably be around 16-years-old, they'd never have been to a 'house' party before so didn't know what to expect and they'd always be sat, totally ashen-faced by around 9pm as random people set about destroying the family home (the hysterics would already have come and gone).

Somersall, Walton, Ashgate and Brookside were normally the 'must visit' parties as the pads were normally sprawling and rife for larceny and vandalism on a grand scale.

Paul Hand, better known as Poggy and these days proud owner of Moor Food on Whittington Moor, was probably more streetwise than many but it made little difference

DIRTY STOP OUTS' GUIDE TO 1980s CHESTERFIELD

when word of his own gathering hit the streets. He turned to drastic measures to save the family home from being dismantled brick by brick.

He said: "It was Paul Hickman who chucked the waste paper bin from the garden through the bedroom window but at least he agreed to pay the £24 it cost to have a new one put in.

"But it was all downhill after that. When all the food started disappearing from the kitchen and there was black dye all over the doors I totally lost it. I pulled the plug out of the stereo and started threatening people with a kitchen knife.

"My mum and dad were on holiday and as you can imagine were not impressed when they returned, even though most of the mess had been sorted. God knows how many people were there. It's a good job Facebook didn't exist in those days."

Even by today's standards, the 'party' that took place at one enormous house in Somersall took some beating in the mid-1980s.

Hundreds turned up - punks, goths, rockers, trendies and every other youth cult going.

That was one good thing about house parties, they were a true melting pot for everyone and everyone had roughly the same goal - get drunk and destroy everything. People, for once, weren't fighting each other, they were united in mindless vandalism and theft.

I actually think the house that night was empty and awaiting the arrival of its new owners after being sold but the former resident (well the son as far as I remember) wisely hung onto a set of keys.

'Mottie's party' became the stuff of legend.

Paul Hand, who'd obviously learnt nothing from his own experiences, was one of the ones arrested. He said: "I think there were at least three double decker buses from town full of people on the way to the party after the Civic had turned out. I can remember the Brimington punks dismantling part of the building. Getting arrested was a low point for me. Rimmo got arrested and had some girl's knickers in his pocket which he duly handed back to her in the police van."

I've seen less police at a Premiership Football match than the amount that turned up that night. They must have enlisted help from neighbouring forces as there was scores of them everywhere.

Joe Peterson said: "I remember hundreds of people running through the gardens trying to get away from the police. It was totally and utterly mental. There really was some mad stuff that went on that night. Mottie's Party really was the Ground Zero of home entertainment. I think that event actually affected people. There didn't seem to be quite so many after that.

"I went to some absolutely marvellous parties in my youth. They were the cheapest form of entertainment going, no question. The houses would invariably get wrecked. I don't why on earth anyone would ever entertain the idea to be honest."

Parties invariably felt far safer places than your average town centre pub for anyone that was nearing/or had just reached the legal age for alcohol.

It wasn't uncommon for the party organisers to end up locking hundreds outside as things got out of hand and the words "party's over - you can all go home" was repeatedly screamed as everyone carried on regardless.

Joanne Marsh said: "I seemed to end up in some pretty wild and wonderful places where parties were concerned. Most rumours about where they were and when they were taking place invariability ended up being true. I think we must have had a sixth sense in the 1980s. We normally only had half an address and we'd be wandering the streets looking for the vital signs - lager cans in the garden, people stood in the road outside or urinating in the garden.

"If things were a bit more intimate you'd need to get nearer to the house and listen for the music."

The dining room at the Olde House Hotel

DIRTY STOP OUTS' GUIDE TO 1980s CHESTERFIELD

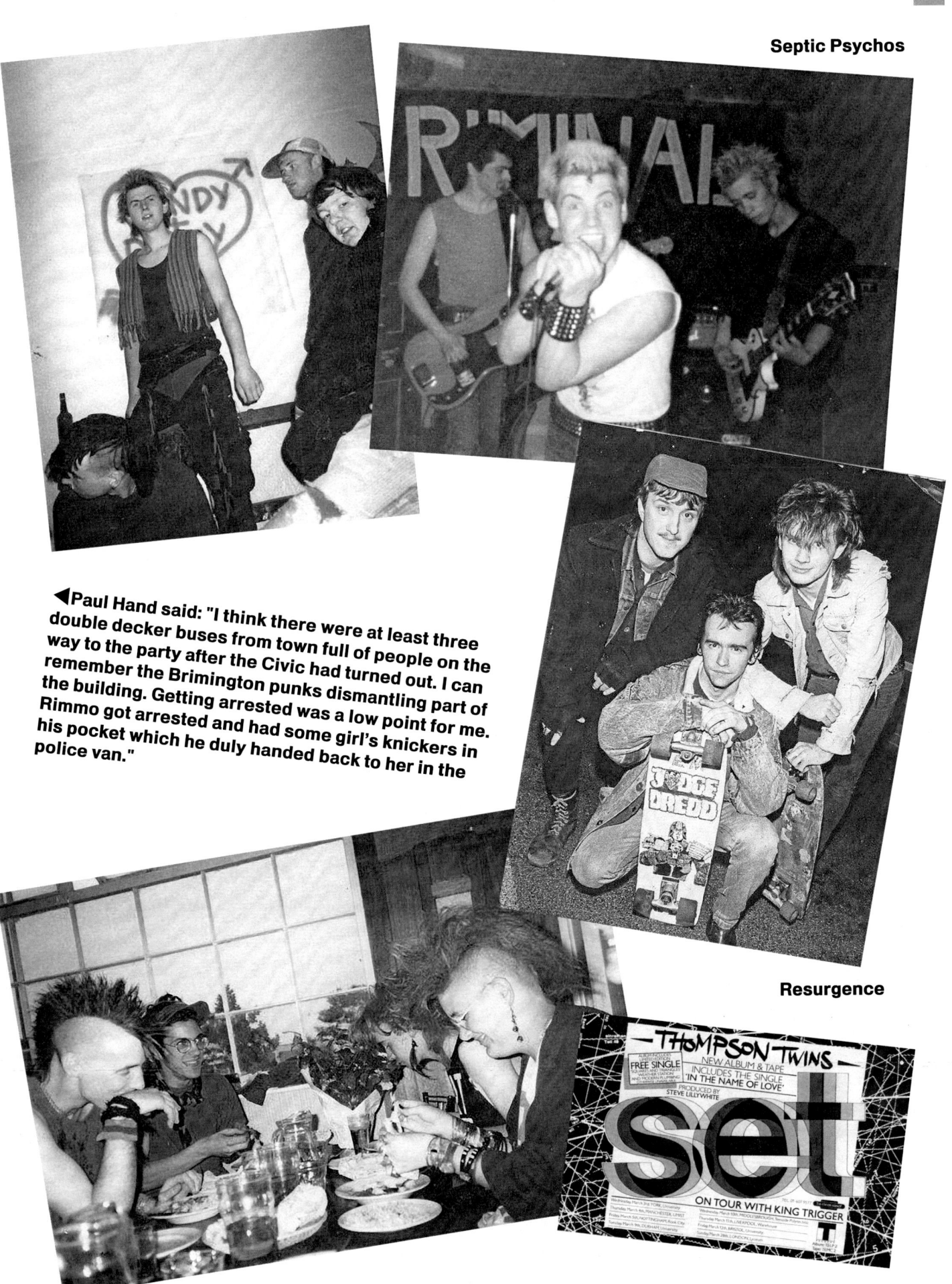

Septic Psychos

◀ Paul Hand said: "I think there were at least three double decker buses from town full of people on the way to the party after the Civic had turned out. I can remember the Brimington punks dismantling part of the building. Getting arrested was a low point for me. Rimmo got arrested and had some girl's knickers in his pocket which he duly handed back to her in the police van."

Resurgence

DIRTY STOP OUTS' GUIDE TO 1980s CHESTERFIELD

◀Nights out could get truly messy - people could, and did, end up in some strange places... Here's a few examples:

Tim Early said: "Police station, lol."

Shaun Stevenson said: "I woke up one Sunday morning in some bloke's house in Dunston, and remember walking home through a throng of wedding guests, and as the bride got out the car, I couldn't keep it down any longer, and threw up over the wall of the churchyard... Classy!"

"On another occasion, there was a knock at my window at 2am. I opened it to find half a dozen girls needing somewhere to stay. This was relatively unusual as I lived in a first floor flat! I had to leave early for work the next morning, so just left them all there. I still don't know who they were... anyone remember this?"

David Malf Palfreyman said: "Somewhere just outside Derby in the company of the ex-wife of a very famous actor."

Malcolm Booth said: "Southport!"

Richard Rodda said: "In a garden near Chesterfield crumpled up at the bottom of a twelve foot wall!"

Tony Martin said: "Bus shelter on Derby Road."

Robert Webley said: "Androo Wobble's house. That mannequin in the bathroom made me jump EVERY time."

John Douglas said: "I was once woken up by a policewoman lying on a pile of snow (me, not her) in Chesterfield bus station."

Iain Jex said: "A bench outside KFC, a corridor at the college, someone's back garden, the Anchor doorstep (woke up by landlord Harvey at 7pm, before all day drinking started), I'm sure there's more..."

Androo Wobble said: "Bit of a session and fell asleep outside Planet X but this was during the day."

Jez Bateman said: "Big holly bush next to the Spire..."

Selmer Truvoice said: "Ralph's house on Newbold Road with Paul Wheeldon, Simon, Kev, Mark Adams etc. It was always unusual although it may have been late seventies rather than 1980s... Does it still count?"

Darrell Taylor said: "Warner Street covered in frost."

Karl Sturmer said: "West Bars Roundabout covered in frost. And when I woke up... I still had a bottle of Thunderbird Gold in a placcy bag! Result!"

Marc Hoyland said: "On a stall on Chesterfield market on a Friday morning after Monty's rock night. Some guy woke me up as he wanted to set his stall up..."

Mark Davison said: "Graveyard on Newbold Road, covered in leaves. Someone from the church woke me up to see if I was ok! lol. Just very, very drunk!"

The unorthodox end to a night out was helped by any number of alcoholic concoctions known only to Chesterfield...

Paul Hand said: "The best was 'loony juice' in the Three Horseshoes, the worst was mine and Mick Johnson's home brewed onion wine, disgusting."

Shaun Dale Ashmore said: "My brother used to go on about the cider in the Horse Shoes. The County did a good pint of Stones. Best home ales, Gladstone at Pilsley."

Mick Johnson said: "'Loony juice' was Coates triple vintage cider. God bless Fred Tipping and the blind pianist and his brother drumming. Also the onion wine was best consumed with Newman after a three day Dexys binge, snowball fight and a

DIRTY STOP OUTS' GUIDE TO 1980s CHESTERFIELD

subsequent visit to the dentist."

Mark Adams said: "I think me and Kris can vouch for Paul and Mick Johnson's home made tea and raisin wine. Cosmic drunk, a whole new dimension."

Kris Kneller said: "If I remember, Mark, it sent us blind..."

Mark Adams said: "We had to meet our girlfriends in the Sun Inn and yes, we were visually at a loss."

Harris Carpets prior to the controversial arrival of McDonalds

DIRTY STOP OUTS' GUIDE TO 1980s CHESTERFIELD

Grassmoor miner Terence Frost who rescued a pensioner from a fire in 1984

David Clarke looking after the Spire Church clock in 1982

DIRTY STOP OUTS' GUIDE TO 1980s CHESTERFIELD

The 1981 Royal visit

◀Kevin Ashcroft said: "The two favourite nightclubs of choice were Fascination which was not always overbusy and playing chart hits and occasional obscure funk and futurist sounds and the night could be rounded off with fish and chips from the nearby Pisces fish bar, which still stands today. The other notable nightclub I remember was The Aquarius based a short taxi ride from the centre of town. The sound of 'Mickey by Toni Basil and anything by Go West bring back fond memories but I was not so fond of leaving a drink on the table unaccompanied as they had a strange habit of disappearing quickly and I don't think it was the magicians that had performed in the cabaret, but the night could be finished off with a delightful burger from the converted ambulance takeaway outside."

◀Wendy Joel said "First proper kiss was at the number 54 bus stop in the station on Vicar Lane. Other memorable spots included a doorway somewhere in the Shambles and the doorway to the Town Hall and in Spires Pub. Plus the churchyard at the back of the Crooked Spire. Wasn't the same after they installed the floodlights though."

◀Dave Berry said: "I bet a lot of people don't remember the Aquarius was also a rock venue. Def Leppard played for two nights when they were getting big. Slade also played there.
"It was a great meeting place for musicians like me. You could be leaving a gig from as far away as North London and still get back there for 1.30am and get a late drink."

DIRTY STOP OUTS' GUIDE TO 1980s CHESTERFIELD

Queen's Park assistant gardener Andy Wade in '85

The Gazette, 14th January, 1988—Page 25

UFO spotted over Brampton

A GROUP of seven people watched in fascination, some of them for almost an hour, as a giant UFO and her "chicks" hovered silently in the skies above Chesterfield.

Afterwards one of the watchers, retired college lecturer Geoffrey Thorneycroft, declared: "There have been so many sightings throughout the world I firmly believe there is another technology, equal to or superior to our own, which is reponsible for these manifestations."

His hour of wonder began as he descended the stairs at his home in Old Road, Brampton. "My wife pointed out a static illumination, glowing green, blue and red - a bit like Blackpool Illuminations," he said.

"She called in neighbours David Wheatcroft, a senior building inspector with Chesterfield Council, his wife and sister-in-law and shortly afterwards I alerted another neighbour and his son. They all saw the big disc-shaped UFO and the three smaller ones."

Mr. Thorneycroft added: "Most interestingly, during the time we watched the UFOs an aircraft proceeded towards the north-west and someone in the plane must have seen what we saw, it was such a clear night.

"Eventually, the angle of elevation of the big UFO changed a few degrees until it went behind the trees to the north of us, although we could still see its brilliance through the trees.

"I could kick myself for not getting the car out and driving to Pudding Pie Hill at Wigley and taking the binoculars with me. It's just that we were all stunned by what we saw."

Mr. Thorneycroft, a lecturer in motor engineering at colleges in Sheffield until he took early retirement at age 55 three years ago, said he telephoned the police to report what he saw.

He went on: "It's not the first time I have seen anything like this. Three or four years ago I was travelling between Heath and Sutton-cum-Duckmanton when I saw three spheres travelling at high velocity across my path and disappearing from north to south."

A police spokesman said: "We gave Mr. Thorneycroft the telephone number of a UFO investigator, as we do with all such reports."

Adam & Eve on Lordsmill Street

Dirty Stop Outs Guide to **1980s** Chesterfield   **AQUARIUS** Edition

A NIGHT AT THE **'ACCA'**

CHAPTER TEN

The eighties weren't kind to Chesterfield. The Miners' Strike split entire communities and the recession hit hard.
But the Aquarius continued to thrive with the emphasis being more and more on its successful disco.

Hundreds would regularly be queuing outside on a Friday and Saturday night.

The venue was packed every weekend.

Even film star Oliver Reid famously turned up one night – he got absolutely hammered!

Brenda Evell: "I loved Thursday night's disco over 21s it was brill just hard to get up next morning for work."

Terry Thacker: "Grab a granny night - it always was a good atmosphere I thought. Some good acts in the main room. Really great **memories**."

DirtyStopOuts.COM

Dirty Stop Outs Guide to **1980s** Chesterfield — **AQUARIUS** Edition

Faces of the Aquarius

Dirty Stop Outs Guide to 1980s Chesterfield **AQUARIUS** Edition

Steven Townsley: "You couldn't be a scruff. It was shirt trousers and shoes and a tie if your wanted entry. Its a shame not all establishments do it now."

Diane Deja: "I had some great nights in the Aquarius! Saw some great acts. Best for me was The Real Thing and remember meeting Oliver Reed. Happy days!"

Rebecca Carley: "Free bus down from town. Chips from the bottom bar. Scran van outside with the biggest burgers ever."

Tracey Sweetie: "Brian the Singing Miner coming on stage on his donkey.... Priceless... Never seen it as packed as that night."

The party didn't start there though. It actually started a few hours before in Chesterfield town centre.

The glitzy Spires – the former Painted Wagon - was regularly the final destination before one of the many corporation buses was boarded to take you to the venue.

> The dancefloor was a sea of white stiletto shoes and handbags being danced around.

A cavalcade of double-deckers – filled with some of the noisiest punters you'd ever find – made the mile or so journey in the direction of Sheffield Road.

Other coaches would regularly bring the hordes from right around the region.

Dresscodes were always strict and collars for men were required as a matter of course.

The dancefloor was a sea of white stiletto shoes and handbags being danced around. Dancemoves were at best pedestrian where the males were concerned and the ladies stuck to half pints of lager and lime.

Paul Michael Sargaent: "I've never told anyone this but I feel now is the time to get it off my chest. My sister had been seeing her boyfriend of the time for a number of years. Many Fridays after seeing her he would offer to give me a lift to the club. My sister thought he was doing me a favour before heading home. But the thing is he was coming clubbing with me. We did this quite a few times over the months. I always felt guilty but I never did grass. Even when I caught him copping off. I guess he wasn't the right bloke for you anyway hey Jo lol?

"I remember '91/'92 and it was the fashion to wear a suit and tie or maybe a waistcoat. There was still quite a strict dress code in clubs. It was all part of the whole getting ready: Music on and sorting the hair out. I was never one for curtain style. I liked it short and gelled. Fahrenheit aftershave or maybe Paco Raban. Gold rope chain and my favourite shoes – gangster-type ones. They looked like bowling shoes but were black and white. I thought I looked the dogs bollox. I probably looked a total cock. There wasn't much choice drink-wise. Either pints or Pils or maybe Diamond White or Newky Brown. Great memories tho - and the fags were so so cheap!!!"

Dirty Stop Outs Guide to **1980s** Chesterfield **AQUARIUS** Edition

74

Toasting the Aquarius

Dirty Stop Outs Guide to **1980s Chesterfield** **AQUARIUS** Edition

CHARITY DISCO
at the
AQUARIUS NIGHT CLUB
Chesterfield
on
TUESDAY, 29th JUNE, 1982
7-30 — 12 midnight

Tickets 60p Each

268

S NIGHT CLUB
Tel.: 70188/9

SENTS

Pitney Show
on
7th FEBRUARY, 1983
be taken by 8-30 p.m.

while Gene Pitney is on stage.

Table No. 55

Dirty Stop Outs Guide to **1980s** Chesterfield **AQUARIUS** Edition

Future Anchor landlord Harvey Hill (left) in the Crown & Cushion

Dirty Stop Outs Guide to **1980s** Chesterfield   **AQUARIUS** Edition

Faces of the Aquarius

Dirty Stop Outs Guide to **1980s** Chesterfield **AQUARIUS** Edition

Dirty Stop Outs Guide to **1980s Chesterfield** **AQUARIUS** Edition

Chesterfield faces of the 1980s – courtesy of the amazing collection of Kathryn Brown

Dirty Stop Outs Guide to **1980s** Chesterfield   **AQUARIUS** Edition

80

Aquarius in the '80s

Dirty Stop Outs Guide to **1980s** Chesterfield **AQUARIUS** Edition

THE END OF AN ERA

Aquarius in its 1970s heyday

The world changed in the 1990s as dance music went mainstream.

Clubs had to adapt to keep going. Many surviving cabaret acts became old hat as a new wave of 'alternative' comedians came to the fore.

Competition got more and more fierce and Working Men's Clubs were falling out of favour. Even dresscodes were starting to become a thing of the past.

> Clubs had to adapt to keep going. Many surviving cabaret acts became old hat as a new wave of 'alternative' comedians came to the fore.

The after dark landscape of Chesterfield changed immeasurably. It was a similar pattern in scores of towns and cities.

Chatsworth Road's Bradbury Club became a massive force to be reckoned with and Xanadu was thriving.

Molly Jordon: "It was a sad day when the Aquarius closed for the last time. I had so many amazing nights in there. So many different ideas were tried to keep the venue going but it could quite shrug off its image as a cabaret and disco club from a different age. It will always be fondly remembered."

Sally Laverick: "The Gate was brilliant. It was as good as any dance club anywhere in the late 1990s. It had some great DJs and really kicked the old Acca into the days of clubbing. It's a shame it didn't last. There only ever seemed to be one side open when I went. It never seemed to reach its full potential."

Clubgoer James Robert said: "There was a massive move towards the newer venues in the 1990s.

The nightscene of Chesterfield changed a lot."

A large percentage of the Aquarius audience were working class – Chesterfield suffered greatly in the aftermath of the Miners' Strike and the decimation of the coal industry.

"Pit closures and a 'dated' image" were cited by the Derbyshire Times as the root of the venue's problems as it fell into the hands of receivers.

All-in-all it was a rollercoaster of a ride for the Aquarius in the 1990s.

At one point it re-launched with a rather more "naughty" image together with Mandy – Chesterfield's first female DJ – and a free 'boozer cruiser' coach that ferried people from the town centre to the venue. Many remember it re-launching as dance club The Gate.

The management seemed to throw everything at it to make it work.

Club Extreme would run on a Friday. Free before 11.30pm, they'd lined up Galaxy 105's Alex Pepper to pull in the punters.

Different nights, different DJs, different promos – The Gate just never got the traction it needed to drag the punters to Sheffield Road like it did in the old days.

Sadly, nothing could save it in the end. The building's still there but its nightclubbing days are long gone.

> Sadly, nothing could save it in the end. The building's still there but its nightclubbing days are long gone.

But its amazing legacy lives on. Friendships were formed that will last a lifetime. It provided a launchpad for aspiring stars that went on to be world-beaters. It entertained generations of the same family and will never be forgotten.

The Aquarius in full swing in the 1970s

ABOUT THE AUTHOR

Neil Anderson first launched the *'Dirty Stop Out's Guide'*™ as part of a PR campaign in the mid-1990s to help regenerate Sheffield's nightlife.
Since then he has written/published a retrospective series that is slowly creeping across the UK.
He has written on nightlife and entertainment for titles spanning *The Independent* to *The Big Issue* and was a *Sheffield Telegraph* columnist for 12 years.

We have been given kind permission to use the Aquarius photos contained on back cover (main shot), front cover (main shot) P1, P3, P6/7, P9, P11, P71, P72, P73, P74 (top), P75 (top), P77 and P80 by copyright holder David Miller. His Aquarius & Talk of the Midlands collection, were recently re-discovered after being lost, and thought to be destroyed many years ago.

Jenny Taylor, who was working on the digital conversion process, was keen to ensure the 'collection' (then several large boxes of random prints and films) was retained because they were a unique record of a very large number of people. Jenny sadly passed away in 2008.

In 2012 many sacks of additional material, thought to be rubbish, were discovered. They proved to be the complete collection of negatives and prints from the Aquarius and the Talk of the Midlands.

We are presently working with David to create a permanent archive. None of these photos can be reproduced without the express permission of David Miller.

Also available now from www.dirtystopouts.com

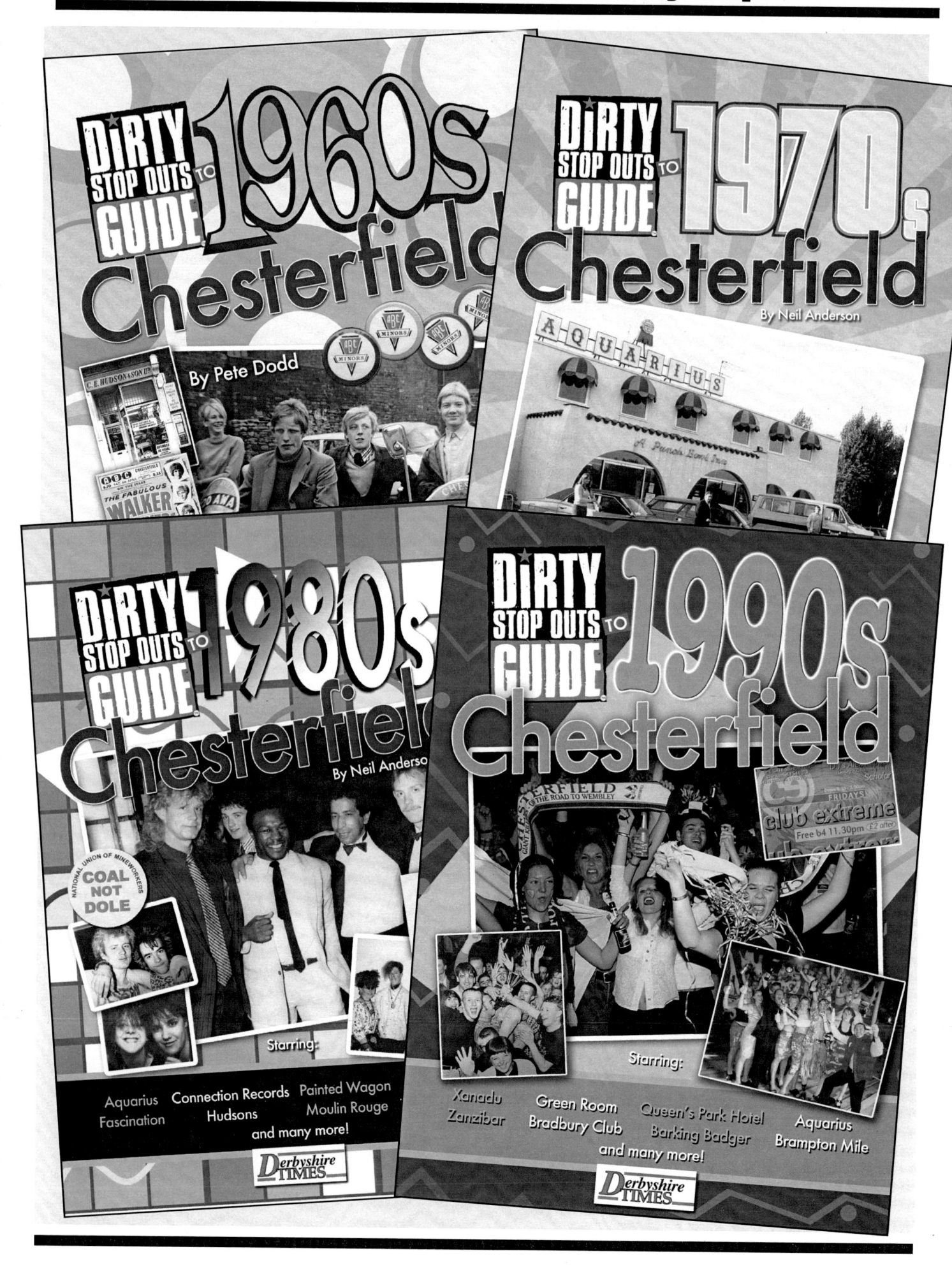